ORGASM EVERY DAY, EVERY WAY, EVERY TIME

ORGASM

Every Day, Every Way, Every Time

A WOMAN'S GUIDE TO SEXUAL PLEASURE

JENNY WOOD

Amorata Press

Published in the United States by
AMORATA PRESS
an imprint of Ulysses Press
P.O. Box 3440
Berkeley, CA 94703
www.amoratapress.com

First published in London in 2007 as *Yes, Yes, Yes*
by Michael O'Mara Books Limited

ISBN10: 1-56975-630-9
ISBN13: 978-1-56975-630-0
Library of Congress Control Number: 2007906078

Printed in the United States by Bang Printing

10 9 8 7 6 5 4 3 2 1

U.S. Proofreaders: Jennifer Privateer, Elyce Petker
Cover design: DiAnna Van Eycke
Cover photo: © photos.com
Interior design and layout: what!design @ whatweb.com
Illustrations: Vanessa Bell

CONTENTS

AUTHOR'S ACKNOWLEDGMENTS

I OWE A HUGE AMOUNT OF THANKS TO:
Victoria White and everyone at *Company* for their help, encouragement, and for suggesting I write "Sex News" all those years ago. Emma Dally and Kate Gribble for their expertise. Vanessa Bell for the late-night discussions on what a Rabbit vibrator looks like. Kate Hodgkison, Catherine Pile, Lauren Crooks, and Rebecca Stening for their research skills. Jill Foster and Louise Wilson for teaching me rude Scrabble. My parents for their never-ending support; and Graeme for not being embarrassed about this book's subject matter. Finally, thanks to Paul Wilson—for everything.

Jenny Wood

PREFACE

YES, YOU CAN HAVE THE SEX LIFE YOU DESERVE

While it's true you don't need to have an orgasm to enjoy sex, let's face it, it's a pretty important ingredient.

Every woman deserves a fantastic sex life, but sometimes, work, stress, communication issues, low self-confidence, health problems—and hey, even men themselves—get in the way. And when that happens, the big O can seem like a distant dream.

That's why this book is solely dedicated to helping you enhance your sexual pleasure, and achieve the ultimate sexual thrill—a mind-blowing, earth-shattering orgasm. By the time you've reached chapter fourteen, I hope you'll be climaxing like a pro, whether that's with a man or on your own.

This book is unique, because it's written purely from your point of view—in every chapter, (readers of *Company* magazine, the top British glossy magazine for women in their twenties,) talk about their experiences, share their successes, and reveal their fail-safe tips for guaranteed ecstasy. Two brave couples have even tried out ten of the most orgasmic sexual positions going, in a bid to make sure you really do get the best advice possible.

So grab a glass of wine, switch off the phone, and start reading. Your journey towards bigger, better, more amazing orgasms starts here!

CHAPTER 1
THE SCIENCE BIT

MY BEST EVER ORGASM...
The orgasm I remember most clearly was my first one. I was twenty-three, and while all my boyfriends had been up for the challenge of making me come, I'd never managed it. I was beginning to think I was abnormal, when a new man—who's now my husband—spent about three hours on foreplay one night. He made me feel like a total goddess, and I was enjoying myself so much, I forgot to get paranoid about having an orgasm. So, when one snuck up on me, I was blown away. I cried afterwards—I couldn't believe how fantastic it was. Since then, I've had many more great climaxes, but that one will always be my favorite!
JESSICA, 29

THE BIG O—WHAT'S THE POINT?

Orgasms are one of life's great mysteries. Both men and women have them, and neither needs a partner to experience them. But whereas men have orgasms for obvious reproductive reasons—their climax results in the ejaculation of sperm, which is needed to fertilize a woman's egg, and produce children—women can get pregnant without orgasms. So, why do we have them at all?

Many experts say that if women didn't enjoy sex, we wouldn't bother with it, and as a result the human race would die out. Perhaps orgasms are nature's cunning way of tempting us to get down to business. But if that's the case, why isn't the clitoris—an essential ingredient in the majority of women's orgasms—inside the vagina, so it can be stimulated only by penetration?

Others say female orgasms are an accident, and the clitoris is just a happy coincidence: just as male fetuses develop nipples in the womb that don't grow into breasts, women develop clitorises which don't grow into penises. This might explain why it's harder to give a woman an orgasm than a man. However, it would also suggest women's orgasms should be less powerful. They're not—male climaxes tend to be over in a couple of seconds, whereas women's orgasms can last up to a minute (lucky us!).

That's why some experts believe our orgasms are linked to reproduction after all. They point out that the rippling contractions of the woman's orgasm cause the cervix to dip down and draw the man's ejaculate up into the womb; then propel it towards the fallopian tubes, where fertilization takes place. The womb also arches and expands during orgasm, making it easier for sperm to enter inside. While scientists aren't 100 percent sure if this helps make conception more likely, it's definitely a convincing argument.

Perhaps the best theory, though, is that orgasms are designed to help us find the right partner, and stick with him—the idea being that only a long-term, intelligent, sensitive, sexually able man will know how to push our buttons. It seems to make sense—during male and female orgasm, a hormone called oxytocin (known as the "love hormone") is released into the bloodstream, making us feel love, warmth, intimacy, and satisfaction. Not only does this make us more likely to want sex again, to experience the same fantastic high, but it can also bond couples together—essential if they are to stay with each other long-term and create a family. Whatever the reason, it's certainly true that if you can find a man who knows how to give you spine-tingling orgasms time after time, you're bound to think twice before giving him the boot!

THE ANATOMY OF AN ORGASM

Let's start with the good news—no two orgasms are alike. The kind of climax you have depends on a huge number of factors, including the method you use to achieve it, the time of the month, your mood, your health, your hormones, and even the person you're having sex with! This explains why some women say reaching the big O is like a series of warm, gentle waves; while others take great delight in telling you theirs is like a full-on internal fireworks display. But whether yours are ice-cream smooth or scream-from-the-rooftops crazy, what's physically happening is exactly the same...

STAGE 1: AROUSAL/EXCITEMENT
This can take anything from zero to twenty-five minutes. Just seconds after foreplay begins, your temperature starts to rise slightly, and your neck and chest may look rosy and flushed. If he's doing the right thing, the tiny Bartholin's glands at the entrance to your vagina begin secreting a mucus-like lubricating fluid. Meanwhile, glands in the vaginal walls also start secreting fluid to get things moving internally—

which is why, if he's just twiddling your nipples as if he's trying to tune in to the radio, your vagina won't feel ready. At the same time, the inner lips of your vagina (*labia minora*) fill with blood, and the whole area becomes darker in appearance. As foreplay continues, your uterus, which normally looks like a deflated balloon, rises up and lengthens, stretching your vagina in preparation for intercourse. Your outer lips (*labia majora*) swell and part slightly, revealing the entrance to your vagina. All this increased blood flow usually means your nipples will harden and, as a bonus, your breasts may even increase in size. Your clitoris also gets pumped up with blood, swelling and hardening.

STAGE 2: PLATEAU

The plateau stage lasts between a few seconds and a few minutes. Now everything is pumped up with blood, your initial excitement levels off, giving you a delicious take-me-now feeling. Your uterus continues to swell, and the top of your vagina keeps expanding. Your clitoris swells and stiffens; if it's being stimulated at this stage, it often becomes ultrasensitive, and may seem to disappear beneath its hood, as it moves back towards your pubic bone to protect itself. But don't worry—you can continue the fab feelings by stroking the sides or around it instead.

STAGE 3: ORGASM

Just as every woman is different, the method of getting her to climax is different too. Whether you climax after clitoral stimulation (known as a clitoral orgasm), or through penetration (known as a vaginal orgasm), the exact biological triggers for the female orgasm are still not known. Some experts believe the sensations from stimulation are sent through the pudendal nerve (which is linked to your clitoris) to the spinal cord and up to the brain, which identifies them as being pleasurable. The brain then sends this message back down to the vulva, causing an orgasm. Others believe the vagus nerve, which emerges from the underside of the brain and runs right down to the cervix, has a part to play. Both theories explain why it's impossible to climax if you're not switched on mentally as well as physically, and why you'll never get there if you're doing it while trying to follow an episode of *Law & Order* at the same time.

During an orgasm, your uterus rises and the upper part of your vagina swells outward. The muscles in and around the vagina and the orgasmic platform (the tissues inside your vagina, near the entrance) begin to contract quickly, causing deliciously pleasurable sensations. Usually, you'll experience between three and twelve quick pulses, lasting about a second each, before the contractions slow down and the feelings slowly disappear. Some very lucky women find that, if stimulation continues soon enough after an orgasm, they can have another one fairly quickly—the infamous multiple orgasm.

STAGE 4: RESOLUTION

As the contractions of orgasm fade, the excess blood quickly drains away from your pubic area, and your uterus and clitoris return to their original positions. Your vaginal lips will revert to their normal color within seconds, and sadly your boobs return to their usual size, although you may be left with a slight flush on your face and chest. Your temperature and heart rate also return to normal. And if you're really unlucky, your man will take all of these as his cue to turn over and go to sleep!

THE KEY TO ORGASM: YOUR CLITORIS

Scientists used to believe the clitoris was just a little button of sensitive tissue—but we now know it's just the tip of the iceberg, the top of a huge collection of nerve endings, which run down either side of your vaginal lips and into your inner thighs. For most women, it's not an optional ingredient in their orgasm—apparently, a whopping 75 percent of women need their clitoris stimulated, either through thrusting during intercourse, or by touching with fingers or a tongue, to tip them over the edge. So, if your man doesn't know where it is, it's time to take him on a personal tour!

How do I find it?

Part your outer lips and focus just above your vaginal opening. The clitoris looks like a tiny pea, covered by a hood of skin.

Still can't see it? Lie down, with your legs relaxed and apart. Begin by exploring your outer vaginal lips and the surrounding area with your fingers—rubbing, stroking, pressing, and experimenting until you find the most pleasurable techniques. Concentrate your movements around, and then directly on, the area towards the front of your vagina. Keep up a steady rhythm, and, as you get more excited, the clitoral hood will retract, and you'll see it in all its glory!

Can women have erections?

In a way, yes. As you become more aroused, your clitoris and vagina get pumped up with blood, causing them to swell and redden. Scientists used to think this was because women are delicate flowers, and their vaginas need to be protected from the force of a man's penis during sex, but it's now thought the swelling occurs to open up the entrance to the vagina, making it easier for a penis to enter—and to increase the woman's pleasure at the same time.

If most of my clitoris is inside me—how do I reach the rest of it?

Just as your man's penis has a head and a shaft, so does your clitoris. The shaft is a slim bundle of muscles, which begin inside your body, curve up above your clitoris in a U-bend shape, and then end in the visible clitoris outside your body. So, if you're feeling adventurous, rather than simply concentrating on the clitoris itself, explore the area around and, particularly, above it—you may be surprised by how good it feels.

MALE VERSUS FEMALE ORGASM—WHAT DOES YOURS FEEL LIKE?

VICKY, 25, HAS BEEN WITH HER BOYFRIEND FOR FOUR YEARS. SHE DESCRIBES HER ORGASM:
I need a huge amount of stimulation before I reach climax. That's probably why my very first orgasm was one I gave myself. It took several weeks of practice, and it's taken years to perfect my technique—in fact, I'm still learning now. I've never had an orgasm with a one-night stand—the only man to give me an orgasm is my current boyfriend, and he did it the first time we had sex. Maybe that's why we're still together!

Having said that, I get aroused fairly easily. I begin to feel little tingles in between my legs almost as soon as my clitoris is touched. If it's then rubbed with a fairly steady rhythm, and a firm but gentle pressure, this tingling continues, and I get wet down below within seconds. As the tension builds, my clitoris gets sensitive, and I don't like it to be touched directly—I much prefer a flat hand over all my vagina, moving in a soft circular motion.

As I get nearer to orgasm, my breathing gets shallower, and I feel myself getting hotter. My boobs swell, my nipples get hard, I feel my vagina swelling, and I get even wetter. The anticipation is almost unbearable—but in a good way. I can't guarantee I'll orgasm, though—sometimes I'll get to the edge, but never quite tip over; I'm not always exactly sure why, but sometimes it's because I'm not totally relaxed, the pressure or touch changes at the crucial point, or I get distracted and the moment is gone. If I think it's going to be difficult, I can often help things along by rocking my pelvis up and down, or squeezing my muscles inside.

When I do finally orgasm, it's amazing. There's nothing better. I know it's going to happen a couple of seconds before it hits me. The world around me seems to disappear, I get a kind of rushing in my ears, and then the contractions hit. They're really powerful—I usually get six to eight big ones, and then my clitoris will pulse, very gently, for up to two minutes afterwards. If I'm in the right mood, I can come for a second time almost straight away—but I can usually only do this when I'm on my own, as I have to rub really hard and at just the right pace. It's never as long or as intense as the first one, though. My boyfriend is very patient, and he loves making me come. He's able to make me orgasm both with his hand and his penis, but while I often come with him inside me, it's usually because my clitoris is being rubbed in some way. When we first got together, if I didn't orgasm for some reason, he'd feel a bit of a failure, but I told him that's just the way we women are!

ADAM, 30, HAS BEEN WITH HIS GIRLFRIEND FOR SEVEN YEARS. HE DESCRIBES HIS ORGASM:
For me, the sensation starts within my body, where my dick and balls are. It's really hard to describe the exact feeling I get—it's like a kind of warmth, or something welling up inside me. I always know when I'm about to come—not because my balls rise up closer to my body, although I often see this happen, but because a couple of seconds beforehand, something in my brain just clicks, and I know I've reached the point when I can orgasm.

During orgasm itself, I get hot down below, and I can feel a kind of pulsing, as if sperm are shooting up from my balls and being pushed up and out the top of my dick. Sometimes, especially if it's been a long time coming, my butt and legs will shake, too.

It's good watching your sperm squirt out—in fact, it's spectacular. I love seeing how much I've produced and how far I can shoot it! My girlfriend says she loves to see it too. For that reason, my favorite place to come is on my girlfriend's boobs.

Afterwards, I often feel light-headed and wobbly for a few minutes, and my penis gets sensitive. It's true what they say about men getting sleepy after climax—I feel an enormous sense of relaxation; the way you'd feel after a good, strenuous workout.

I find orgasms during sex are different to when I masturbate. Most men have been giving themselves orgasms for years before they even get near a woman. You know you can do it, you know exactly how to do it, and it's fairly functional—maybe you do it because you're bored, or you've just got a hard-on. But climaxing during sex is different. When I masturbate, I can make myself come within minutes, whereas during sex I can hold off for a while. I've heard that some men are two-second wonders and come almost immediately, while others—okay, so they're probably porn stars—can keep going for hours. I'm somewhere in the middle—I like to try to satisfy my girlfriend first. I'm good at controlling my orgasm. I never find myself thinking, "Get on with it, I need to come"; I'm more likely to think, "Get on with it, my hand is tired!"

I've gone from one long-term relationship to another, but I can understand how some men, if they haven't had sex for a while, might be selfish during a one-night stand, and just do whatever they need to climax, regardless of the woman's pleasure. After all, you're never going to see her again, so you might as well enjoy it. That might sound cruel, but I bet a lot of women think the same thing. I think sex in a relationship, or sex with someone you've had sex with a few times before, is better, because you know a bit more about each other in bed, and it's miles more fun if both people are enjoying it.

There's no such thing as an "okay" orgasm—they're all incredible. But some are definitely better than others. However, I don't remember specific orgasms as such; I'm much more likely to remember the place and the situation and, of course, the person I was having sex with! I find one of the best things about sex is giving my girlfriend orgasms. It's a pride thing. If you've had sex and you've both come, you lie there with a big smile on your face—you're physically and mentally pleased. Even though men's orgasms are good, they're pretty easy to achieve, whereas all men know it takes skill to give a woman one. Seeing my girlfriend smiling, and knowing it's because of me, that's the best thing I can do in bed.

OVER TO YOU...

Every orgasm is different, so I asked five women to describe the feelings they get at the point of no return:

It's one of the few things that make me speechless! I get a total adrenaline body rush—a surge of sensation and then an incredible release. Afterwards, I feel completely exhausted. It definitely ensures I get a good night's sleep!
      DONA, 25

I get this amazing tingly feeling, and then my whole body feels like it's burning up, until I get to the point where I think I just can't take it any more.
      KAREN, 25

It's different every time, but the best way to describe it is I feel like a little volcano waiting to erupt—sometimes it takes ages, and I just have continuous pleasurable feelings; other times, the feelings surge up and down, which I suppose is a multiple orgasm. Then there are times when I'm so damn excited that

the volcano erupts really quickly! Normally, if I rest, then start going again, I can get a second orgasm soon afterwards.
YASMIN, 28

I get a very hot flush all across my body—my cheeks burn and my vagina starts to throb so much it becomes tender. My body starts to jerk, and then, at the end, I go extremely dizzy and get very wet. It's so intense my body usually rises slightly off the bed when I come.
MICHELLE, 26

My orgasms have the same intensity you get when you need to go for a pee—but the best way to describe it is the feeling you get when you tickle yourself until you shiver!
EMMA, 30

CHAPTER 2

DISCOVER YOUR PLEASURE POTENTIAL

My best ever orgasm...
A friend told me her man asked if he could watch her pleasure herself. She obliged, and discovered she loved it. I thought I'd be too self-conscious, but the next time things were getting steamy with my boyfriend, I took the plunge and started touching myself. The thrill of seeing him turned on and knowing what I was doing, meant we both had amazing orgasms!
Louise, 24

ORGASMS—CAN EVERYONE HAVE ONE?

If films, television, magazines, our men, and even our friends are to be believed, orgasms are every woman's basic right. If you're not coming every which way, every time you have sex, there must be something fundamentally wrong with you, right? Well, no, actually. The truth is, even the most orgasmic women find that, sometimes, reaching climax is as easy as squeezing yourself into a pair of skinny jeans three sizes too small—no matter how hard you try (or how much lubrication you use!), it's just not going to happen. Understanding this is the key to getting the sex life you want.

Don't believe me? To bust the myth that all women should orgasm all of the time, a British woman's magazine, *Company*, launched a survey to find out exactly what twenty-something women felt about the big O. The results were fascinating, surprising—and very reassuring. While most women said they had experienced an orgasm at least once in their lives (either alone or with a partner), contrary to popular opinion, only a lucky quarter of women claimed they climaxed every single time they had sex. A further 23 percent orgasmed every other time; a realistic 23 percent said they orgasmed only "every few times"; 14 percent said they rarely reached the big O during sex; and an extremely honest 12 percent admitted sex has never ended in climax for them at all.

For women, reaching orgasm is not an exact science. While men find climaxing as easy as ABC (accelerate, brake, come), sex for women is an entirely different experience. We need to be switched on both mentally and physically to reach the peak of sexual excitement, and every woman has a slightly different way of getting there. For example, when *Company* asked women how they reached climax, 32 percent of them said they needed to be totally relaxed and have tons of very specific foreplay; while a further third said they could come only in certain positions. Vibrators worked for 17 percent, while another 17 percent said they needed to fantasize during sex in order to help tip themselves over the edge. All this goes to prove there are no right or wrong ways to go about reaching orgasm—and what works for one woman may be a complete turnoff for another.

So, forget what you see in Hollywood blockbusters. It's time to stop seeing orgasms as the Holy Grail—a goal to be achieved at all costs. The harder you focus on and chase after an elusive orgasm, the more your enjoyment of the physical sensations during sex slowly ebbs away—leaving you feeling stressed, let down and, ironically, completely orgasm-free. That's why, instead of feeling like a failure if you can't reach orgasm every time, you should start realizing that the journey there—the beginning and middle of any encounter—can be just as, if not more, satisfying than the end result. Enjoy the tingle you get when your partner kisses your neck; soak up the feelings of intimacy and closeness that you get from being naked with the one you love; and revel in the sensations of having your man inside you. In a way, taking this approach is likely to make you more orgasmic, because the best orgasms happen when you least expect them.

WHAT'S YOUR PLEASURE POTENTIAL?

In the *Company* survey, a whopping 46 percent of women were dissatisfied with the number of orgasms they were currently having. Of these, 13 percent felt frustrated; another 13 percent claimed the lack of orgasms didn't bother them in the slightest; 3 percent felt inadequate; 2 percent were actively upset; and a huge 21 percent said the amount of orgasms they were getting wasn't ideal, but they lived with it. But a less than satisfactory sex life is not something you have to put up with. While you'd be forgiven for thinking your orgasmic style is set in stone—and if you've always found it difficult to reach the big O, that that's just the way you were made—this isn't the case at all. It's also untrue that if you're already a red-hot, multiorgasmic lover, there isn't room for improvement. With an open mind, a little bit of effort, and a lot of practice and patience, you can up your orgasm quota significantly.

You've taken the first step by picking up this book; now, whether you're already a tigress in bed, who enjoys orgasms that leave you feeling on top of the world, or you're a pussy-cat who's not even sure she's had an orgasm at all, this quiz will help get you started on your journey of sexy self-discovery...

1. IF YOU SOMETIMES HAVE SEX WHEN YOU DON'T FEEL LIKE IT, WHAT'S THE MOST LIKELY REASON?

A. You know that once you get going, you'll warm up and start to really enjoy it.

B. Your man wants to have sex, and while you're not in the mood, you don't want to disappoint him.

C. That never happens—you always feel like having sex.

D. You end up having sex because you need some love and affection.

2. FOR YOU, WHERE DOES FOREPLAY PHYSICALLY START?

A. With a relaxing back rub, holding hands, or other nonsexual contact.

B. When your breasts and vagina are touched or stroked.

C. As soon as you know you're going to have sex, you start to feel turned on.

D. Once you begin kissing.

3. GETTING MORE INTIMATE, WHEN DO YOU MASTURBATE?

A. Usually when you're on your own, but you sometimes ask your man to help you climax.

B. You've only done it a few times, and you were always alone.

C. Either alone or in front of your partner, as it really turns you both on.

D. Only when you're alone and won't be disturbed, like in the bath or bed.

4. DO YOU EVER HAVE ORGASMS IN YOUR SLEEP?

A. You think you might have climaxed during erotic dreams, but you're not entirely sure.

B. No, you don't think you ever have.

C. Yes, definitely.

D. No, but sometimes you have raunchy dreams where you're having sex.

5. ARE YOUR SEXUAL FANTASIES...

A. Buried deep in your memory, but very real and physical once you conjure them up?

B. Romantic and dreamy, with sex as the end of the scenario?

C. Always one or two thoughts away, and you can get very quickly turned on by thinking about them?

D. Varied, and sometimes you fantasize you're making love to someone else when you're with your partner?

6. DO YOU RECOGNIZE IF OR WHEN YOU ACTUALLY NEED SEX?

A. Yes, you think you have needed it sometimes, but you don't have any signs you regularly recognize.

B. You don't think you ever actually need sex.

C. Yes, your body tells you when you need it.

D. Kind of—you get really cranky and tense if you don't have sex for a while; then you feel much better afterwards.

7. IS AN ORGASM AN ALL-OVER BODY EXPERIENCE FOR YOU?

A. Yes, after climaxing you tingle all over, from head to toe.

B. Sometimes it feels like your whole body was involved, but you're not always exactly sure it was an orgasm.

c. Yes—and you can have an orgasm by touching your breasts or other parts of your body besides your genitals.

D. No, but you do feel it very intensely in and around your vagina.

8. HOW DO YOU HANDLE STRESS?

A. You lock the bathroom door and have a hot bath with lots of posh, pampering beauty products.

B. You allow yourself time to unwind alone, often listening to music or just relaxing.

c. Easily. You treat yourself by indulging on a massage, facial, or body treatment.

D. You often find it hard to switch off—a night out with your friends usually does the trick though!

9. HOW MUCH DO YOU AND YOUR MAN DISCUSS YOUR SEX LIFE?

A. You might initiate a quiet chat over a drink if you feel things aren't going too well.

B. Never. You don't need to discuss it.

c. You talk lots during sex, telling each other what feels good.

D. Not much. You never talk about sex outside the bedroom.

10. WHICH OF THE FOLLOWING SUMS UP HOW YOU MOST REGULARLY FEEL DURING SEX WITH YOUR MAN?

A. Connected and content.

B. Attractive and loved.

c. Sensual and horny.

D. Desired and involved.

HOW DID YOU SCORE?

MOSTLY As

You're a very open and affectionate lover. You have few psychological or physical hang-ups about sex, and have been known to experiment when you feel like it. You need and enjoy foreplay, and go for men who are more than willing to spend time over your body before going for the main event. However, you may not realize just how orgasmic you can be. Try talking to your man a bit more in bed—at the moment, you tend to save the sex talk for times when there's a problem, instead of emphasizing the positive side of things. Remember, men can be just as unsure of themselves in bed as women, so they love to be told when they're doing things right, and how good they're making you feel. Sharing your fantasies could also be a revelation for you—find out what yours mean in chapter eight of this book. On the whole, though, you're at a really exciting stage in your love life—your sexual confidence is growing, and you're ripe for new experiences. Why not test out some of the positions in chapter six, and let your bedroom personality, and your orgasmic potential, develop even further? You could be in for a few wild surprises!

MOSTLY Bs

Like many women, you're probably not sure if you've ever had a "proper" orgasm. This is very common and nothing to panic about, as it's the pressure to have orgasms that often stops them happening in the first place. The fact is, 99 percent of women are orgasmic—it just takes some of us longer to discover this than others.

Your answers show that you feel sexy and attracted to your partner, but find it hard to make the mind/body connection. You're also so busy trying to please him that your own pleasure often ends up on the back burner. You love the intimacy of a sexual relationship, but may think great sex is a natural thing that happens automatically, and if you haven't got "it," well, that's just tough. The truth is, sex isn't separate from the rest of your life, and it requires the same thought, work, and determination you give to the rest of your pleasures. Great sex takes patience—hot, first-time romps can't sustain a relationship for very long; you also need trust, relaxation, and lots of courage. On the other hand, settling for a relationship with too few sexual thrills might lead to heartbreak later on. Glitches in your sex life need to be talked about and dealt with if both of you are to fulfill your bedroom potential.

Remember, though, every woman and every orgasm is different—some describe their orgasms as intense, others say they're more like soft ripples. To find your own physical peaks of pleasure, first sort out any problems by reading chapters ten and eleven; then explore your erogenous zones with a little help from the tips in chapter five; and set yourself some foreplay homework with chapter four. Perhaps most importantly, turn to chapter seven to learn how to turn yourself on through masturbation, as the key to having orgasms with your man is often first to learn how to give them to yourself. Once you recognize orgasms when they happen, you'll be on the way to the sex life of your dreams.

MOSTLY Cs

You're definitely orgasmic and you enjoy it to the max. You probably already experience powerful climaxes that you can feel throughout your whole body, and this makes you feel very sensual and in control. This is good news, but at times you may be so sexually confident that affection and intimacy take a backseat. While it's great to push back the sexual boundaries, your demands for excitement might make you an intimidating partner, and could mean you're easily bored in long-term relationships. To prevent this, and really reach the peak of your sexual powers, you need to put in some extra effort. Share your knowledge with your partner; if you know cunning ways to get to an instant orgasm, show him. It might turn him on and will definitely help your communication with one another about your sexual needs. In-depth discussions can also boost the intimacy in your relationship, which can lead to real mind/body orgasms. Looking for ways to take your orgasms up a level? Try the tips in chapter thirteen.

MOSTLY Ds

You occasionally climax when making love, so you're definitely orgasmic, but you've got the potential to enjoy sex so much more than you do at the moment. Presently, an orgasm is the icing on the cake for you, not part of the mix. You know how to get there, but sometimes you just can't (or can't be bothered?). You play it safe, having sex only when you really feel like it, possibly preferring the same route to pleasure every time. You're missing out on some great erotic opportunities. Why not let your partner persuade you to make love on the spur of the moment? Make him make you want him!

It's also worth remembering sexual pleasure doesn't have to start down below. It's far more exciting to build an orgasm through contact with other parts of the body, so try thinking of (and using) your whole body during foreplay to boost your pleasure and confidence—read chapter four for inspiration. Try trusting your own sensations more—it can be easy to imagine other women's orgasms are more exciting, which can leave you disappointed with your own. You may also find it hard to ask for what you want in bed because having desires seems slightly embarrassing to you. Don't be ashamed of exploring your sensual side—get to know your body and its responses with the tips in chapter seven. A satisfying sex life will soon be yours!

OVER TO YOU...

Need more proof that the best orgasms hit you out of the blue? I asked five women to reveal the methods of reaching the big O that surprised even them...

After a long day at work, I got home one night to find my man had filled the bedroom with candles. I hadn't noticed the tabletop fridge until we were at it, and he suddenly reached over and placed something cold between my legs. It was an ice cube, and the cold against my hot skin felt incredible. I came so quickly, and it took me ages to recover. Who knew ice could be so sexy?
    SOPHIA, 20

I'd never orgasmed with a man until I got together with my current partner. We'd been friends for years, so when we finally took things further one night, I wasn't nervous, which probably helped. He sat in a chair, while I straddled him, and then he just stroked and kissed my breasts for what seemed like hours on end. I couldn't believe it when I came—

he hadn't touched my vagina at all! His total dedication to foreplay is probably the reason why we're now married...

    JENNIE, 29

Whenever I've seen phone sex in films, it's always seemed mortally embarrassing to me. But one night, I went away with work and my new man phoned my cell late at night when I was in my hotel room. He started by asking me what I was wearing (my work suit!) and then described what he'd like to do if he was there with me. At first, I felt really awkward, but then I started to relax and really got into it. Having him talk me into an orgasm was incredibly erotic, and now whenever I go away on business, we'll schedule a late-night booty call—it makes sure I get a good night's sleep afterwards, that's for sure!

    LUCY, 26

I'd been seeing my boyfriend for three years and sex had become routine. So, one day I went to a sex store and bought myself a porn film, vibrator, and massage oil. I thought I had the house to myself, so I put the film on, got comfortable, and tested out my vibrator. Then my boyfriend suddenly walked in! To say he was shocked is an understatement, but he was also aroused. We had mind-blowing sex, I had a fantastic orgasm, and it gave our love life a huge shake-up.

    KERSTIN, 23

I'm a curvy size 18, and while I'm fairly happy with my body, I've always been shy in the bedroom. I used to insist on having sex in the pitch-dark at all times. That is, until I met my current man. The first night we slept together, every time I turned the light off, he leaned over and switched it back on again! He gave me so many compliments; I soon relaxed and had my most powerful orgasm ever. Now, I actually prefer doing it in daylight.

CLAIRE, 23

CHAPTER 3
YOUR ORGASMIC MONTH

My best ever orgasm...
The best orgasm I ever had was after I came back from a girls-only holiday. I'd left my boyfriend at home, and as I'd shared a room with my friends for two weeks, I hadn't even been able to, um, indulge in any solo sex. I don't know if it was the waiting that did it, or just the time of the month, but by the time I got home to my boyfriend, I was begging for it. I walked in the front door, dumped my suitcase, and we made love right then and there on the stairs. I was so turned on I came within minutes. I've never managed to orgasm so quickly since—now I can't wait for my next trip away!
Yasmin, 26

HARNESS THE POWER OF YOUR HORMONES

Ever wondered why one day you feel you could happily seduce sexy Simon from accounts—and all his colleagues—on your lunch break, while others the only action you're interested in is snuggling up in front of the TV in your PJs?

It's because sexual moods and needs are affected by all kinds of factors—tiredness, your emotions, your relationship... and chemicals called hormones, which buzz around your body throughout your menstrual cycle. This means, in the twenty-eight or so days of your monthly cycle, it's perfectly natural to have twenty-eight—or more—different sexual cravings. Hormones not only dictate your emotional moods, they're also responsible for deciding what kind of sex you want, so learning how yours work could be the key to maximum orgasms...

YOUR 28-DAY ORGASM PLAN

Starting from day one of your menstrual cycle (the first day of your period), here's how to work out how to have the kind of sex your body needs, every day of the month.

DAYS 1 TO 5

GREAT FOR SOOTHING SEX

For many women, the start of your period can actually be a relief. You're not pregnant, your premenstrual bloated stomach has eased slightly, and you feel generally calmer, as your levels of both estrogen (the most important female hormone, which affects your mood) and progesterone (the hormone linked to annoying PMS symptoms) are low. If you're unlucky enough to suffer from cramps during your period, having sex can be an enjoyable (albeit temporary) cure, as having an orgasm releases soothing, feel-good endorphin chemicals into your system. Well, it's more fun than taking a couple of painkillers!

Sexy suggestion: If you're skipping sex during your period because you're worried it might get messy, you could be missing out. The extra lubrication your body produces during this time will benefit both you and your man, and you might be pleasantly surprised at how good it feels—and how quickly you reach climax. One of the most comfortable positions for this time of the month is with you both lying on your sides, facing each other or with your back to your man: neither puts any pressure on your stomach.

DAYS 6 TO 8

GREAT FOR SLOW, INTIMATE SEX
Your libido steadily increases when your period finishes. This is because your ovaries are starting to produce more estrogen. Also, you'll no longer feel as tired, crampy, or moody as you may have felt during your period, so it's time to celebrate—with some bedroom gymnastics.

Sexy suggestion: Book a hotel and treat yourselves to a saucy weekend—or just lock the doors and have one at home. Now's a great opportunity to treat yourself to all your favorite sexy things, from massages and bubble baths with your man, to oral sex. Take your time exploring each other's bodies, and working out what turns you on—and off. It'll stand you in good stead for the next few days...

DAYS 9 TO 11

GREAT FOR NAUGHTY SEX
Your estrogen levels are rising fast now, causing your womb lining to thicken in preparation for a potential baby. This means you'll be looking gorgeous and feeling very sexy indeed, so make the most of your natural glow by vamping it up in the bedroom.

Sexy suggestion: Take advantage of your newfound body confidence by trying out some different bedroom moves—particularly ones with you on top. Stuck for inspiration? Why not work your way through the top-ten orgasmic positions in chapter six of this book?

DAYS 12 TO 13

GREAT FOR QUICKIE SEX

Just before you hit ovulation, your cervix starts producing more mucus, which, while it sounds gross, is actually a good thing, as it lubricates your vagina. This is because your body is busy doing everything it can to make sure that when you do have sex, it's as easy, painless, and enjoyable as possible. Chances are, you'll be thinking about sex a lot more right now—and hopefully, having a lot more of it, too!

Sexy suggestion: As your body is ready for action at any moment, foreplay isn't as much of a necessity at this time of the month as it usually is—which gives you the perfect excuse for a quickie. Make good use of your man's, ahem, morning glory, and start the day with a bang—get into your favorite position (the sky's the limit as you're so naturally lubricated) and help things along by rubbing your clitoris with your fingers while he moves inside you. In the evening, why not go for a repeat performance? Just take things a little bit slower this time.

DAY 14

GREAT FOR RAMPANT SEX

It's ovulation time—when an egg is released from one of your ovaries, and travels down one of your fallopian tubes towards your womb, ready to be fertilized by his sperm. So, unless you're hoping to get pregnant, you'll need to be extra careful with your contraception at this time of the month.

Your estrogen levels have reached their peak, and your body also secretes tiny traces of testosterone—the so-called male hormone—to get you even more in the mood. It's not surprising we feel horniest around this time—it's nature's way of ensuring our brain and body are ready for action, maximizing the chance of conception.

Sexy suggestion: At this time of the month, you'll be up for getting down to it wherever and whenever you can. So, tonight's the night to release your inner dominatrix. From the moment your man walks in the door, grab him, plant a huge, powerful kiss on his lips, and inform him that you're in control! This is your chance to tell him exactly what you want, and how you want it, so whether you've always harbored a secret desire to make love on the kitchen table, or enjoy having fast and furious sex with your clothes still on, just go for it. He'll be more than happy to indulge you!

DAYS 15 TO 18

GREAT FOR FOREPLAY

What goes up must come down—your estrogen levels are starting to decrease, while your levels of progesterone are on the rise again. So, while you won't be feeling sex-less, you won't want to be as rampant as you were during ovulation (and let's face it, if you were that frisky all the time, you'd be permanently exhausted!).

Sexy suggestion: Your man is going to have to work extra hard at the moment to get you in the mood, which means you get to be the center of sexual attention. In other words, he has to touch your boobs and vagina more gently than usual, sensuously cover your body in kisses, and generally do all the things you love in bed. You could even give penetrative sex a miss altogether and suggest he brings you to climax with his fingers, tongue, or a vibrator. Bliss!

DAYS 19 TO 25

GREAT FOR SLEEPY SEX
Your progesterone levels are still on the up, which means your PMS symptoms may be increasing too. Chances are, you'll be feeling a little irritable, tearful, tired, clumsy, and frankly not very sex-goddess-like at this point in your cycle.

Sexy suggestion: Instead of having arguments with him over why he never puts the garbage out or notices the towels aren't lined up perfectly, instigate a big hugging session, which leads to tender, minimum-effort sex. You're tired, so you don't want anything too complicated—go for the Spoons position (see page 83), where you lie on your side, while he lies behind you and enters you from behind. As long as you're lubricated enough (natural or from a tube, it's up to you), you don't need to do a thing. And the best thing about this position? You don't have to move a muscle afterwards, and can drift off into a contented, satisfied sleep.

DAYS 26 TO 28

BEST FOR PAMPERED SEX
You're about to get your period and your body's probably feeling swollen, tender, and bloated. Your estrogen levels are low, so your libido is hitting rock bottom. But that doesn't have to mean a sex ban...

Sexy suggestion: At this time of the month, you need to feel as pampered as possible—before, during, and especially after sex. To get yourself in the mood, have a long, candlelit bath together, and ask your man to give you a gentle shoulder massage. When you feel relaxed and ready for the next stage, let him carefully dry you with a soft towel and lead you to bed. The most important thing to remember with premenstrual sex is to do it slowly, so your body has plenty of time to prepare itself. In the bedroom, take your time to heat things up—treat each other to some oral sex before penetration, and for afters, get him to hold you until you fall asleep. Perfect.

YOUR SEX-DRIVE HIGHS AND LOWS

If life was like the movies, you'd wake up leisurely every day, turn over and have great early-morning sex; then come home at night for a repeat performance on the living-room carpet. In reality, the only button you want pressing most mornings is the snooze switch on your alarm clock; and when you get back in at night, you'd rather collapse on the sofa in front of the television than get down to business on the carpet. This doesn't mean you've got a problem—in fact, it's more likely to mean you're human! It's natural for your libido to have highs and lows, especially if you've been in a relationship for a long time.

So, what exactly is a "normal" sex drive? In a *Company* magazine survey, 85 percent of female readers in relationships claimed to have sex at least once a week, with 35 percent of those claiming they get down to it more than three times a week. Only 3 percent of women in relationships had sex less than once a month; compared to 59 percent of single women. But if none of these statistics sound like you, don't worry—the best and only real way to define whether your libido is normal is if you're satisfied with the amount of sex you're wanting or having.

If you're not satisfied or you've gone for weeks without feeling horny when you're normally up for it at least once a day, it might be worth looking into why. Don't panic, though—researchers at University College London Medical

School suggest up to half of all women experience sexual problems at some point in their lives; and a flagging libido can be caused by all kinds of factors, many of which are easily fixed. Here are the five biggest sex-drive killers—plus five top ways to put the buzz back into your sex life...

TOP-FIVE SEX-DRIVE KILLERS

THE PILL

Some women find the combined Pill can seriously affect their desire to have sex. The main problem is that the Pill raises the levels of a substance called sex hormone binding globulin (SHBG), which stops the male hormone testosterone in your body from doing its job. As testosterone helps increase blood flow to your vagina, and improves sensitivity down below, it's unsurprising that without it, you'd rather bake a cake than have sex. As well as affecting your testosterone levels, some Pills suppress your ovarian hormones, which may send your sex drive plummeting, although scientists are still working out how. Alternatively, it could just be because the Pill keeps your hormone levels stable throughout your cycle—rather than giving you the rollercoaster urges you get during normal ovulation and menstruation—so you feel less in the mood for sex on the Pill than you do off it.

Your action plan: Each Pill has a different combination of hormones, and there are dozens of different formulations, so talk to your doctor about changing brands. Or you could try another form of contraception that doesn't rely on hormones at all, such as condoms, a copper coil, or a cap. But don't just assume your low libido is caused by the Pill, particularly if you've taken the same one for a long time without any problems. It could be your sex life has got into a bit of a rut, in which case, you need to talk to your man.

STRESS

Tiredness and stress are your libido's biggest enemies—if you're worrying about debts, meeting work deadlines, or the argument you've just had with your mom, sex will be the last thing on your mind. When you're stressed, you also release high levels of the hormones cortisol and adrenaline—cortisol affects your levels of testosterone; while adrenaline diverts blood flow away from your vagina. Put this all together and it's no wonder you don't feel horny!

Your action plan: Funnily enough, when you're stressed, having sex is the best thing you can do. Not only does it release feel-good hormones, such as oxytocin, which help bring down your stress hormone levels, but it helps clear your mind, giving you the mental and physical break your body is craving. If you honestly can't face sex after a long day in the office, and are regularly too tired to feel even slightly saucy, you need to take a good long look at your work/life balance. Try to get into a regular sleep pattern, take up a form of exercise (whether that's relaxing yoga or tension-busting kickboxing!), and work out what conditions you need to chill out and enjoy sex. If you're too exhausted when you get home from work, try morning sex instead—or if weekdays are too busy, opt for a lazy Sunday session.

ANTIDEPRESSANTS

Around a third of the people who take selective serotonin reuptake inhibitors (SSRIs)—newer types of antidepressants—have problems with their sex drive. As well as dampening libido, other possible side effects include difficulty in reaching orgasm—or not being able to reach it at all.

Your action plan: Don't stop taking any drug without talking to your doctor first. You've got several options, such as swapping to a different type; taking an extra drug to counteract the side effects of the antidepressants;

decreasing your dosage slightly; or waiting a few months until your body has built up a tolerance to the drug, and the side effects die down. Talking to your man is very important in this situation, too—it would be easy for him to think he's the problem. Try to inject some romance into your relationship, agree a new rule that foreplay or cuddling doesn't necessarily have to lead to full sex, and be patient. Sometimes, you might not think you want sex, but after a bit of gentle foreplay (and lots of sexy massages from your man), you may find yourself pleasantly surprised as your body kicks into action.

RELATIONSHIP PROBLEMS

Whether it's something minor, such as a fight over who does the dishes, or something potentially life-shattering, like one of you having an affair, anger and resentment are the biggest libido-killers going. Good sex—or in fact, any sex at all—is about enjoyment, relaxation, and letting go, so if you're harboring a grudge, it'll seem like a chore. If you don't address your relationship problems, days without intimacy can turn into weeks, and before you know it, lack of sex has become just one more thing to argue about.

Your action plan: All relationships need a bit of nurturing every now and again, and until you've got whatever's bothering you out in the open, it's likely you'll be uninterested in sex. Sit down together and let each other speak—air your grievances and really listen to what the other one has to say (that means no sulking, storming off, or smashing china). If you really find it difficult, you might want to consider seeing a couples' counselor to help get the ball rolling. Once you've both got everything off your chest, avoid a repeat performance in the future by trying to set aside quality time with your man at least a couple of evenings a week. Spend it relaxing together, sharing a bottle of wine, or simply chatting. Who knows where it might lead?

MEDICAL CONDITIONS

Thyroid problems, diabetes, high cholesterol levels, and high blood pressure can all kill your libido, by messing with your circulation, nerves, and hormone levels. Anemia—particularly common in women with heavy periods—is another culprit. Put simply, it's a deficiency of red blood cells, which carry oxygen around your body. A shortage of oxygen in your blood can make you feel tired in a can't-be-bothered-to-do-anything way, and can slash your desire to get down to bedroom gymnastics.

Your action plan: Boost your iron levels by eating more meat, eggs, iron-fortified cereals, and leafy green vegetables like spinach. You could also ask your pharmacist for a good-quality iron supplement. If this doesn't help, let your doctor know your sex drive has taken a knock, and ask for a general checkup, to be on the safe side.

TOP-FIVE LIBIDO BOOSTERS

EXERCISE

If your libido's flagging, it could be time to dust off that gym membership. Burning calories outside the bedroom has been proven to get you in the mood for sex, as exercise releases feel-good chemicals, called endorphins, into your bloodstream. Long-term, exercise improves your energy levels and stamina, helps to balance your hormones, and also has a positive effect on your body image—all of which add up to an increased desire to get down to business.

Your action plan: There's no getting around it, you need to start working out. But you don't have to toil for hours on a treadmill—any kind of activity that gets your heart pumping and your body sweating will do. If you can't stand gyms, try exercise classes; squash or tennis; running; swimming; or team games instead. Ask a friend, coworker, or even your man to be your exercise buddy, so you can motivate each other, and aim for at least three twenty-minute sessions a week. You should start to see, and feel, the benefits within weeks.

HERBAL REMEDIES

Certain herbs have been used for centuries to help boost both male and female libidos; although very few have been proven to work in clinical trials, fans of these natural remedies say they've transformed their sex drives. The most famous ones include Dong Quai, used in Eastern medicine to regulate hormones and improve blood flow; Damiana, an ancient aphrodisiac from Mexico said to improve sexual desire; Muira Puama, discovered in the Amazon and used to treat exhaustion, strengthen the nervous system, and ease menstrual cramps; Ginkgo Biloba, which is supposed to increase circulation and comes from the leaves of the Maidenhair tree, one of the oldest living plant species; and the fantastically named Horny Goat Weed, used in China for over 2,000 years to increase testosterone levels.

Your action plan: While herbal remedies might seem harmless enough—and many are a lot of fun to try—they can interfere with certain medications, like the Pill and antidepressants; or affect medical conditions such as high blood pressure. It's also not a great idea to mix several different herbal remedies at once. So, proceed with caution—always consult your doctor or pharmacist before taking any natural remedy, and if you experience any unusual side effects, stop immediately. Looking for a good place to start? Try evening primrose oil—less scary than many other remedies, it's widely available in health stores and pharmacies, and is often used to balance hormone levels, which in turn can get your libido back on track. Be patient, though—herbalists claim you'll need to take it for a few weeks before you see a difference.

APHRODISIACS

Named after Aphrodite, the Greek goddess of love, the definition of the word "aphrodisiac" is "anything which arouses sexual desire." Over the centuries, much has been claimed about the aphrodisiac qualities of certain foods, such as caviar, bananas, oats, vanilla, mangoes, and oysters (Casanova was said to eat fifty a day to keep his stamina up), but the jury is still out as to whether they really do boost libido—or if they work only because you want them to. However, it's certainly true that some of the best-known aphrodisiacs contain vitamins and minerals that can help your sexual health. Oysters contain more zinc—which helps to keep your testosterone supplies topped up—than any other food; chocolate contains phenylalanine, a substance which triggers feel-good endorphins, your body's natural antidepressants; while saucily shaped asparagus (think about it!) is high in vitamin E, which is often thought to boost sex hormones and vaginal lubrication.

Your action plan: Test out the claims by planning an aphrodisiac meal for you and your man. To start, it has to be oysters; followed by zinc- and iron-rich steak with asparagus; with a rich chocolate mousse for dessert. For a racy treat, don't use plates for the final course—lick or kiss it off each other's bodies. Whether chocolate works as an aphrodisiac or not, you'll certainly have fun finding out!

A BALANCED DIET

Good nutrition is vital for a healthy mind, body, and sex life. If your body doesn't have all the nutrients it needs to function at its very best, it stands to reason your libido's going to suffer. Mineral, vitamin, and other nutritional deficiencies can lead to hormone imbalances, nerve and organ problems, energy dips, and poor circulation—all of which can spell trouble for sexual desire. Scientists have also discov-

ALCOHOL—SEX-DRIVE BOOSTER OR KILLER?

Ever wondered why some women say a drink or two makes them super-horny, while others find they can't reach orgasm after a glass of wine, no matter how hard they try? Well, even experts aren't really sure! In one piece of research, 60 percent of women surveyed claimed alcohol helped them shed their inhibitions; 45 percent said they found it made sex more pleasurable. However, some scientists reckon these libido-boosting effects could all be in our imaginations. When female volunteers watched an erotic movie when sober, most of them said they didn't feel very turned on; yet when they were given two or three drinks, they claimed to feel much "hotter." Yet signs of physical arousal, such as increased blood flow and vaginal secretions, proved their sexual responsiveness was actually lowered after the drinks, and

heightened after the film. This might explain why having more than a couple of drinks can mean we take longer to reach orgasm—our minds are willing, but our bodies aren't.

On the upside, though, the same piece of research found that although orgasm can take longer to reach when we're a little tipsy, we enjoy it more when it happens, perhaps because we've lost our hang-ups.

The other theory involves our hormones. Small amounts of alcohol can cause a huge, temporary surge in testosterone levels, and therefore sexual desire. The effect is apparently strongest in women who are ovulating or on the Pill, as they have lower testosterone levels to start with.

Whatever the reason, it's certainly true that if you believe you're sexy, you'll feel sexy. So if having a glass of wine makes you enjoy sex more, go for it!

ered being overweight can affect your libido—losing even a few pounds through a healthy diet and exercise plan could kick-start your sex hormones back into action.

Your action plan: Stock your cupboards with libido-friendly foods. Try to get a good mix of protein (from cheese, nuts, and lean meats like chicken) and complex carbohydrates (such as wholegrains) every day; plus fill up on tons of fresh fruit and vegetables. Want to target a specific problem?

To balance your blood-sugar levels, go for chromium-rich meat and whole-grains; for energy, go for vitamin B-packed foods like brown rice, cereals, fish, and dairy; to boost your sex-hormone levels, opt for foods rich in antioxidant vitamins A, C, and E, such as leafy green vegetables, fruit, nuts, and seeds; to improve circulation, eat onions and garlic; and to raise your testosterone levels, eat shellfish, pumpkin seeds, and chicken, which are chock-full of zinc. Still want more? Ask your pharmacist for a good multivitamin supplement, but remember, it's no substitute for the real thing. Oh, and if you really want to see results, try cutting down on alcohol, coffee, and cigarettes too—they undo all your hard work by destroying vital nutrients and dampening desire.

EROTICA

Need a little help in the bedroom department? Stimulating your brain—often called your biggest sexual organ—by watching or reading about sex can be a huge turn-on: getting you in the mood mentally, and preparing your body for the real thing. This doesn't have to mean hard-core porn—you might find a really sexy scene in an otherwise perfectly respectable film or a saucy passage in a bestseller will do the trick just as well (if not better).

Your action plan: Discover what turns you on. Erotica has a bad reputation, but it's very different to top-shelf porn—the classy stuff is in a league of its own. Saucy rather than smutty, there are now hundreds of sexy stories written for women by women; and even female porn directors making hugely watchable films which focus on the woman's pleasure, rather than the size of the man's equipment or the leading ladies' silicone beach balls. Not sure where to get started? Look for the erotica section in your local bookshop or an online bookstore; ask for advice in a sex store like Good Vibrations; or visit a female-friendly sex-toy website, for reviews of books and DVDs. Once you've found something that presses your buttons, think about sharing it with your man. It's unlikely he'll complain!

OVER TO YOU...

Your cycle is unique to you, so I asked five women to reveal how their libido affects their orgasms:

The week before, and the week after my period, I get more sexually charged than usual. It doesn't affect whether I have an orgasm or not, but I definitely come more quickly than normal.
    IOLANDA, 27

My menstrual cycle has a major effect on my libido. I get so horny the day before my period arrives—I can guarantee that I'll always have an orgasm!
    KAY, 25

The likelihood of having an orgasm is always pretty good, but I definitely get more randy at different times in my monthly cycle; when that happens, my orgasms go through the roof! The first day of my period is the only time I'm not usually in the mood, though, as I get really bloated.
    DONNA, 28

I don't have a particularly high sex drive, but every month, like clockwork, I'm desperate for sex the day after my period ends. I don't know if it's because of my hormones, or just because I'm no longer feeling grotty, but I'm definitely up for it and raring to go!
    LOU, 29

Being on my period makes me want sex so much more, and it definitely boosts my orgasms. At other times, when my libido is low, it takes me longer to reach orgasm, and they're much less intense.
    MICHELLE ANNE, 26

CHAPTER 4
JUST FOR STARTERS

MY BEST EVER ORGASM...
Sex never used to be mind-blowing until I read an article
which said it's important to tell your man exactly what you
like and want. So the next time my boyfriend, Luke, and I
were getting busy, I told him I loved to be kissed all over,
and that the more time we spent on foreplay, the better my
orgasms were. Now he spends ages just nuzzling and teasing
me—it's bliss.
   CARRIE, 20

FOREPLAY—WHY YOU NEED IT

Foreplay is like warming up before a workout. It's easy to
skip it, but if you do, your body won't be ready for the main
event, and you definitely won't get the best results. It's not
an issue when you start a new relationship—you both enjoy nothing more than kissing, cuddling, and exploring
every inch of each other's bodies. But as time goes on, the
initial dizzying lust passes, you both assume you know
what the other one wants in bed, and before you know it,
all that delicious foreplay has gone out the window, to be

replaced by a quick kiss and a halfhearted, five-second nipple-tweak.

Part of the problem is we women take, on average, twenty minutes or more to get sufficiently aroused to have an orgasm, while men can be ready for action in minutes. Okay, so quickies can be fantastic every now and again, but the truth is, if you want more satisfying, orgasmic sex, prolonged foreplay is vital.

It's easy to feel embarrassed or selfish asking your man to slow down, but you shouldn't. While the starting point of arousal is the same for both sexes—blood begins pumping around our bodies—the effects are hugely different. For men, the blood flow quickly heads for his penis, giving him the first twinges of an erection, and focusing feelings on his genitals. As the tip of his penis is packed with nerve endings, it's no surprise most men want to stimulate it as soon as possible—preferably by putting it inside you.

For women, however, the sensations that develop are much more complex. After kick-starting vaginal lubrication, the blood flow makes a woman's whole body—not just her vagina—much more responsive to touch. That's why, when he strokes your inner thigh, or kisses your boobs, it can feel electric. Scientific tests have shown that when it comes to skin sensitivity, even the least sensitive woman is more sensitive than the most sensitive man. No one's sure whether this is a physical or mental thing—but the fact remains, we're built very differently to men when it comes to getting ready for sex.

Once you understand this difference in the speed of sexual arousal, the reason why women need tons of foreplay becomes obvious. Many men wrongly assume women are aroused in the same way they are, so they make a beeline straight for your clitoris, hoping to claim their prize. Women, on the other hand, can't understand why their lover is racing through sex instead of lingering over her entire body. No wonder we often both end up frustrated!

So, the message is clear—there's no such thing as spending too much time on foreplay. And that means everything from whispering suggestive sweet nothings in your ear and getting undressed, to kissing and oral sex. Not only will you enjoy the whole sexual experience more if you indulge in a lavish first course, but you'll also be more likely to orgasm. And once your man gets his head around this, you're laughing (and gasping).

YOUR THREE-STEP PLAN TO GETTING MORE FOREPLAY

No one wants to be told their sexual performance is less than perfect. How should you go about telling your man you want more foreplay? The answer is, very carefully—and cunningly...

CHOOSING YOUR MOMENT

Discussing foreplay immediately after sex, when your man is basking in a postcoital glow, feeling great about his bedroom prowess, isn't the best way to start the conversation. He's likely to come down to earth with a swift bump, and be too hurt or angry to listen properly to your point of view. So, instead, bring it up outside the bedroom—during a romantic dinner; when you're curled up together on the sofa; or even while you're busy doing the dishes. Not sure how to broach the subject? It might help to talk about it in a roundabout way. Perhaps tell him you've read about a fantastic new foreplay technique in a magazine; take him to see a particularly raunchy film; read out a sexy passage from a novel; or describe a saucy dream you've had, which featured tons of foreplay, and "joke" that you'd like to try some of the same things one day. Who knows, he might have some similar suggestions of his own...

GIVING HIM THE HINT

Actions speak louder than words, so if his hand's almost-but-not-quite in the right place, don't be afraid to gently move it up or down until it hits the right spot. You can also let him know when he's doing something you enjoy—moan, groan, and generally give him encouragement, perhaps saying something like, "Yes, that's it, don't stop!" to drive the message home. He'll be so pleased with your response, he'll want to do it again next time—and hopefully strive to get an even better reaction by trying out some more, similar moves in the future.

TALKING ABOUT YOUR FEELINGS

Admitting to your own thoughts and feelings about sex can sometimes be a great starting point for a discussion. For example, if you find giving blow jobs difficult or awkward, tell him, and ask for some pointers. Hopefully, he'll then confess he'd like some tips when it comes to pleasing you, too. It's also worth remembering that it takes two to have great sex—if you want him to fine-tune his foreplay, you need to be prepared to fine-tune yours as well. The really good news is that foreplay is all about experimentation, and there are no rights or wrongs—anything goes as long as it turns you on (and it's legal!).

THIRTY FANTASTIC FOREPLAY TIPS

Great sex is all about the buildup. But it can be difficult to know where to begin—or, if you've been together a long time, how to move things on a step. If you're looking for inspiration in the bedroom, try some of these thirty (count 'em) orgasm-guaranteed teasers—sex will never be boring again...

1. GET YOUR PENS OUT.
Draw tiny numbers on your four favorite hot spots—anywhere on your body—from your toes to the nape of your neck. Then challenge your man to find them in the correct order, by using only his tongue. When he does, ask him to spend at least five minutes stimulating each area. By the time he reaches spot number four, you should be fired up and ready to go!

2. OPEN YOUR MAKEUP BAG.
Lip-plumping products or mint lip balms, which make your lips swell and tingle, can have a similar effect on your nipples. Dab a little on, then lie back and enjoy!

3. SWAP HIS FINGERS FOR HIS PENIS.
The head of a man's penis is one of the softest, silkiest spots on his body, so if your man's fingers are rougher than industrial-grade sandpaper, get him to stroke you—on your nipples, inner thighs, and vagina—with his helmet instead.

4. STOCK UP ON FOREPLAY FOOD.
At the supermarket, load your shopping basket with sexy ingredients. On your return, get him to feed you strawberries

with his fingers, tease your nipples with frozen grapes, and drizzle runny honey on your thighs before licking it all off. Yum!

5. EMPLOY HIM AS A MASSEUR.

Put a towel on your bed, hand your man some massage oil, then lie down while he straddles you and gets busy with his hands. If he has a tendency to, um, cut to the chase a little quicker than you'd like, put on a sexy CD, and tell him he can't touch your vagina until the third track's finished!

6. HAVE A STOMACH RUB.

Before things get too steamy, get him to rub and press down on your abdomen gently (that's about 2.75 inches below your belly button). This should help stimulate the blood flow to your clitoris and vagina, making you feel deliciously tingly and ready for action.

7. RENT A SEXY FILM.

Forget dodgy porn videos—get in the mood by renting a Hollywood movie with a sexy plot instead. Try *9 1/2 Weeks* (for the famous midnight-feast scene); *Bound* (if you want some tasteful girl-on-girl action); or *Betty Blue* (the saucy opening scene lasts for ten whole minutes!).

8. TURN HIS PENIS INTO A VIBRATOR.

Slip a vibrating cock ring (from sex-toy websites or sex shops) over his penis, switch it on, and get him to rub it all over your boobs and vagina. It'll feel fantastic for both of you, and as the batteries usually last for twenty minutes, you can make an extra rule—he's not allowed inside you until the time's nearly up!

9. TURN UP THE HEAT.

Soak in a warm bath together, take a jacuzzi, or even do some exercise before having sex. The heat will get your blood pumping and relax your muscles ready for the main event.

10. WATCH YOURSELVES IN A MIRROR.

If you've ever tried having sex in front of a mirror, you'll know just how difficult it is—you're jiggling around too much to appreciate it properly. But watching yourselves during foreplay is an entirely different matter—the slow, sexy moves make great viewing for you both.

11. READ A BEDTIME STORY.

Read aloud to each other from an erotic story compilation—Cleis Press publishes some great titles that contain just the right level of sauciness. Alternatively, write your own sexy stories and read them out to each other while you're naked. Bet you don't get past the first few lines!

12. BREAK OUT THE LUBRICANT.

The next time your man is kissing your nipples, get him to rub a dollop of lubricant lightly onto the one he's not licking. It'll feel like he's kissing them both at the same time. Genius.

13. USE RIBBED CONDOMS.

Ask your man to give you a delicious alternative massage by putting on a ribbed condom and rubbing the ridges over your vagina. If he likes, he can also use massage oil, but because this rots the rubber, make sure he pops on a new condom before entering you.

14. MAKE LIKE STING.

Fans of tantric sex say staring deep into each other's eyes before and during sex helps promote feelings of trust and intimacy—essential for orgasms. Sit down opposite each other and lock eyes for ten minutes, without saying anything. Your hands can wander where they like, but try to keep away from the obvious parts for as long as you can.

15. TRY AN ORGASM-ENHANCING GEL.

It may sound terrifying, but it's very similar to lubricant—just slightly more tingly. Pop a blob on your clitoris and the menthol it contains will draw blood into your vagina, heating them up, and making his every touch feel more intense. Buy a tube from a sex shop or online sex shop.

16. CRACK OPEN THE CHAMPAGNE.

Buy a small bottle (or a large one if you're feeling frisky!) of champagne, and take turns pouring it on to each other's bodies, then licking it off. Get him to dribble it over your nipples, while you lick it off his penis—it tastes fantastic, and the little fizzy bubbles work wonders!

17. SUCK EACH OTHER'S LOWER LIPS WHEN YOU KISS.

The ancient Hindus believed our lower lips were linked to our genitals—so starting up here could help get your motor running down below.

18. GET UP CLOSE AND PERSONAL BY ASKING HIM TO SHAVE YOU DOWN BELOW.

Not only is shaving deeply intimate, but fans of the bald look say going bare down below increases sensitivity—you'll be able to generate more friction during sex, which means your clitoris gets more action. One word of warning—only hand him the razor if he's sober!

19. PLAY A GAME.

It may sound silly, but sexy board games (from sex shops or online sex stores) can break down your inhibitions faster than any bottle of wine. They usually start off innocuously, with questions about your partner's likes and dislikes; then get steadily hotter, ending up with instructions like "Massage your partner's genitals." It's the perfect excuse to try new things.

20. ENJOY A DIFFERENT TYPE OF BLOW JOB—BY GETTING HIM TO BLOW, VERY GENTLY, ON TO YOUR CLITORIS.

He should never blow up your vagina (it can cause dangerous air bubbles), but light blowing further up your genitals can feel amazing.

21. TAKE A BATH TOGETHER.

Okay, so there's not much room to move when there are two of you in the tub, but that's partly the point. It's all about slow, small, sexy movements. Grab a bar of unscented soap, and carefully wash each other all over, paying plenty of attention to your genitals. By the time you've dried off with big, warm, fluffy towels, you'll be more than ready to head to the bedroom to finish things off.

22. EXPERIMENT WITH TOUCH.

Instead of sticking to one technique, ask your man to alternate his stroking with tiny butterfly kisses and very gentle nibbles. The change in sensation will get the nerve endings in your skin fired up in no time, ready for the excitement to come.

23. GIVE YOUR MAN YOUR VIBRATOR.

Using it on the lowest setting, get your man to use it to stimulate your nipples, neck, and even your lips. Just remember to go slowly—if it's too intense, ask him to hold the vibrator over the back of his hand, so the vibrations travel through his fingers. A dollop of lubricant will make it feel even sexier.

24. MAKE FRIENDS WITH THE FREEZER.
We all know ice cubes and blow jobs are a good idea, but what about your pleasure? Get your man to rub one all over your sensitive spots during foreplay—paying particular attention to your boobs and nipples. Delicious!

25. GO COMMANDO.
Go to work without underwear, and tell your man you're doing it just before you leave in the morning. Your mind will be focused on your vagina all day long (as will his); by the time you get home, you'll both be up for the sex of your lives!

26. GET TWICE THE FUN.
It's a myth that men can't multitask. Ask him to use his hands in different ways—perhaps one hand could stroke around your clitoris, while the other gently teases your inner thighs; or maybe one hand could softly cup your left breast, while the other plays with your right nipple. It'll feel like you're in bed with two men rather than one. Well, a little fantasy never hurt anyone!

27. IMPROVISE.
Feathers feel fantastic when brushed lightly over your skin, but let's face it, they're not the kind of thing most people have lying around the house. A soft paintbrush, makeup brush, or even a pastry brush can feel just as—if not more—sexy.

28. INDULGE IN SOME LIGHT BONDAGE.

Don't panic—it doesn't have to involve leather or chains. Any kind of scarf will do—just get him to tie your wrists very loosely to the bedposts, and then kiss you all over... even the ticklish parts. You'll be unable to resist, and can concentrate on the sexy sensations without worrying about having to return the favor.

29. DO IT IN THE DARK.

Turn the lights off, both put on a blindfold, then touch, stroke, and kiss each other all over. Because you can't see, your other senses will be heightened—plus, you'll have the added excitement of not knowing which body part is going to get attention next.

30. ROLL THE DICE.

Cover two dice in plain stickers, then on one, write down six parts of your body, like thighs, stomach, and neck. On the other, write down actions, like stroke, lick, and kiss. Take turns rolling them together, and if you end up getting nibbled on the bottom, don't say you didn't see it coming!

YOUR MAN'S ULTIMATE GUIDE TO ORAL

Oral sex can be the perfect way to get your body firing on all cylinders. Done well, it feels fantastic either on its own, or as preparation for penetration. The only problem is, most men, bless 'em, need a little help when it comes to down-there diving. So, leave this page of the book open somewhere your man will see it. Who knows, he might learn something!

The Basics

1. Do the groundwork. Don't head straight for her clitoris with all guns blazing. Pay attention to all of her lower body—including her lower stomach and inner thighs. Think slow and sensuous licks and kisses, rather than full-on slurping.

2. Get into the groove. If it helps, carefully open her vaginal lips with your fingers first, to expose her clitoris. Now, keeping your tongue as flat as possible, gently but firmly run it up and down her genitals, slowly increasing the pressure. Kiss her vagina like you'd kiss her mouth—varying between sucking and long, sexy licks.

3. Practice your alphabet. A top oral-sex tip is to imagine you're writing the alphabet with your tongue all over her genitals. Skim her clitoris lightly every time you dot your "i"s or cross your "t"s. She won't be able to predict your moves, making the whole thing even more exciting.

4. Hit the spot. Listen and watch out for subtle clues, and once she's ready, start to flick her clitoris from side to side, using your tongue. Then take it in your mouth and wind your tongue around it in little circles. If it gets a good response, you could try a little bit of suction, too.

Advanced Moves

1. Nose dive. Use your nose instead of your tongue—pressure from the bony ridge can feel fantastic.

2. That's handy. To get her juices flowing, play with her nipples, tease her thighs, stroke her stomach, or press the bit of smooth skin between her vagina and anus, while you're using your tongue on her vagina.

3. Ice, ice, baby. Sucking ice, or drinking mint liqueur, champagne, or hot tea before going down will add extra excitement.

"DO"s AND "DON'T"s

Do:
Dart your tongue in and out of her vagina.

Hum with her clitoris in your mouth. It might seem weird, but it works!

Avoid lockjaw by alternating your mouth with your fingers.

Wrap your arms around her bottom and hug her close.

Don't:
Use your teeth.

Stop when she's near climax—you'll undo all your good work.

Be shy—get your whole face involved.

Take her groans to mean she wants you to go faster—she doesn't. She wants you to carry on exactly as you are.

OVER TO YOU...

I asked five women to spill their ultimate foreplay secrets—and they didn't disappoint!

I always thought porn was a man's thing, until I read an article about a female porn director, called Anna Span. I bought one of her films online, to spare my blushes, and, after initially feeling a bit uncomfortable, it wasn't long before I got turned on. I've since bought more of her films, and shared my secret turn-on with my boyfriend, so now we can watch them together.
Natasha, 29

I love building up the suspense of foreplay. So, I start off really gently, stroking my man's hair, while he does the same to me. The feeling is incredibly sensual and the slow buildup really sends shivers down your spine—way before you get to the main course!

KIM, 23

I wasn't convinced when my boyfriend suggested tying me up as part of our foreplay, but after talking about it, I found myself getting quite turned on by the idea. I went online to a sex-toy website and bought a beginner's bondage kit, which included a soft blindfold and soft wrist- and ankle-cuffs. They were fastened with Velcro, so I could free myself any time I wanted. We've never looked back—in fact, I recently bought an advanced kit!

ELLIE, 28

A great trick is to use your tongue on places you'd never normally visit, like each other's wrists, spines, and backs of knees. Then, to add a naughty twist, we give each other a score, so if you're wildly turned on, it's a ten, and if it's only so-so, it's a four. It's the perfect way to learn how to press each other's buttons.

LUCY, 23

I'm not a kinky person—honest—but a couple of months ago, my boyfriend got frisky while I was doing the dishes. I playfully flicked some soapsuds at him, and he responded by lightly slapping my bottom. I admit, I found it strangely sexy, and told him he could do it again if he liked... Since then, we've experimented a bit more with spanking in the bedroom, and it's become a regular part of our foreplay. Something about the naughtiness of it really gets us both going. But we never hit each other hard enough to leave a mark!

LAURA, 27

Chapter 5
ENTER THE ZONE

MY BEST EVER ORGASM...
My ex taught me to use all of my body for sex—not just the typical hot spots. He'd kiss me from head to toe. I found erogenous zones I never knew existed—like when he nuzzled the backs of my knees! The orgasms I had after those sessions were among the most intense I've ever experienced.
   ANNA, 22

FINDING YOUR FEET, NIPPLES, KNEES...

Many people think the only erogenous zones are your boobs and your genitals, but they'd be wrong. The official definition of an erogenous zone is "a part of the body sensitive to sexual stimulation"—so that means anywhere on your body, from the top of your head to the tips of your toes, can be a hot spot if it feels good when it's touched, stroked, kissed, or licked. The reason for this is our skin is packed with nerve endings, and some areas of our bodies are more responsive to touch than others. It's a bit like having a direct hotline to your genitals—when your e-zones are stimulated, your brain registers the pleasurable feelings, and your body releases feel-good hormones, which help to put you in the mood for sex. The really great thing is, there's no exact science to erogenous zones—they're highly personal, and differ from person to person. That's why some women adore having their earlobes nuzzled, while others go crazy when the backs of their knees are tickled. Alternatively, some women have such sensitive skin they reckon their entire bodies are one huge erogenous zone. Lucky them!

As your e-zones are unique to you, the only way you'll find yours is by experimentation. It can seem a bit silly to stroke your upper arms, your ankles, or your belly button, when you could be concentrating on more tried-and-trusted routes to ecstasy, like your clitoris—but if you don't give it a go, you could be missing out. There are also some hidden erogenous zones, like the G spot and the lesser-known A spot, that are actually located inside your body. Finding them might take time, but it could be the key to better, longer, or even just different-feeling orgasms. So, what are you waiting for? Take the phone off the hook, pull the curtains—enlist the help of a willing man, if you've got one handy—and set off on your own personal mission of discovery.

To get you started, here are the top-ten female erogenous zones, where to find them, and how to get maximum pleasure from them:

THE NIPPLE

WHAT IS IT?

The good news is—you've got two of them! These small bumps of skin, in the center of your breasts, are packed with nerve endings and surrounded by a sensitive ring of darker tissue, called the areola. They contain erectile tissue, which expands when you're sexually aroused, or when they're stimulated or exposed to the cold (hence the "peanut smuggling" look you get on winter days!). Some women find one nipple is more sensitive than the other, and others claim they can orgasm just from having their nipples touched for long enough in the right way. Oh, and forget the myth that size matters—it has nothing to do with how responsive they are—small nipples can be absolutely electric, while big ones may feel hardly a flicker (or vice versa).

HOW DO I FIND IT?
Place one finger on the areola and move it in circles around your nipple—or place two fingers either side of the nipple, so they're almost touching it. Move them back and forth, or open and close them, until the skin gets taut and the nipple becomes hard.

HIT THE SPOT
Most women love having their nipples kissed, stroked, or licked, but for a more advanced technique, get your man to swirl an ice cube over your nipple, then warm it up with his tongue. Alternatively, ask him to place his mouth over your nipple, and purse his lips, creating a kind of vacuum effect. If he then sucks softly in and out, the alternating sensations should feel delicious.

IT WORKS FOR ME!
My nipples became much bigger and more sensitive after I gave birth to my daughter eight months ago. Now, even the slightest touch sends little bolts of electricity down towards my vagina. Running around after a new baby means I'm often too tired for sex, but my husband only has to kiss or suck my

*nipples for a minute or so, and no matter how tired I am,
I suddenly feel in the mood. He's obviously delighted by
this—he used to be a "legs man," but now my nipples are
his favorite part of my body!*

SARAH, 29

THE NECK

WHERE IS IT?
So sexy it inspired its own term, "necking," you may know
the nape of your neck—the soft skin at the base of your hair-
line—is an erogenous zone; but did you realize the whole
of your neck can be incredibly sensitive to stimulation?

HOW DO I FIND IT?
The next time you and your man get passionate, ask him
to run his fingers, tongue, or lips gently up and down, and
along your neck and jawline—then let him know when he
finds the part that sends shivers down your spine.

HIT THE SPOT
Get him to vary the pace by leaving your lips for a moment
and traveling southward, planting little kisses all over your
neck, or blowing softly on the skin around your collarbone.
If you're feeling brave, you could even let him nibble it very
delicately—unless he's a *Buffy the Vampire Slayer* fan, in which
case, steer clear!

IT WORKS FOR ME!
*I only discovered how sensitive my neck is thanks to my cur-
rent partner. The first time he slowly moved down from my
lips to my neck, I thought I was going to die with pleasure. I
don't know why, but for some reason my neck is incredibly*

sensitive—when he kisses me softly there, I get tingly all over, and my toes curl. Foolishly, I made the mistake of telling him this, and now whenever we have an argument, or he wants to get his own way over something, he'll kiss my neck, and I find myself relenting!

Corinne, 22

THE EARS

WHAT ARE THEY?

Apparently, ears have been regarded as an erogenous zone for centuries. Not only are they the gateway to the biggest sexual organ of all—your brain—but thanks to their high concentration of nerve endings, they're also extremely sensitive to touch. Some sexperts even go a step further, and claim your ears fill with blood and swell slightly during sex, in the same way your clitoris does.

HOW DO I FIND THEM?

Ask your man to start by kissing your ears softly, and then lightly blowing on them, or tugging the lobes very gently with his lips or teeth. But don't worry if it does nothing for you—some women love having their ears played with like this, while others hate both the feeling and the noise!

HIT THE SPOT

Turn things up a notch by encouraging him to alternate his kisses with low, saucy whispers of exactly why he loves turning you on. That way, he'll be able to stimulate both your body and your mind at the same time—excellent!

It works for me!
I know some people can't bear to have their ears fiddled

with—in fact, my ex used to hate it—but I can't get enough of it. My favorite thing is when a man runs his finger very lightly in circles over the folds, or covers his teeth with his lips and gently sucks my earlobes during sex. It makes me feel incredibly naughty and wanton—like I'm a scarlet woman in a passionate Hollywood love scene.

    CLAIRE, 28

THE FEET

WHAT ARE THEY?

Okay, so they're not the prettiest of body parts, but millions of foot fetishists can't be wrong! The skin on your soles is densely packed with nerve endings, and particularly responsive to touch—meaning a foot massage can feel surprisingly sexy when done the right way...

HOW DO I FIND THEM?

Give your feet a wash in warm, soapy water, then enlist the help of your man. Give him a bottle of massage oil and set him to work rubbing and kneading your soles, paying special attention to your sensitive arches and toes. To discover exactly what presses your buttons, he should experiment with both gentle strokes and firmer pressure, using both his fingers and his thumbs. He can adapt his technique should you find it too ticklish—and dissolve in spasms of laughter!

HIT THE SPOT

It might sound slightly freakish, but toe-sucking (or "shrimping" as it's sometimes known) can be highly erotic. Ask your man to kiss and lick slowly up and down the sole of your foot, before popping your toes in his mouth, one at a time, and pulling on them gently. You'll either love it or hate it—but one thing's for certain, you'll never know until you try!

I love it when my husband gives me a foot massage. I'll sit on the edge of the bed, while he kneels before me—it makes me feel incredibly loved and pampered. He uses tons of baby oil, and pays attention to every inch, from my ankles down to my toes. He knows exactly which areas to concentrate on, and how hard to press. It's the best way to relax after a long day at work, and it really puts me in the mood for sex afterwards.
   FI, 27

THE WRISTS, ELBOWS, AND KNEES

WHERE ARE THEY?
The soft areas on the undersides of your wrists, elbows, and knees are sensitivity hot spots, as the skin here is particularly thin, meaning the nerve endings are nearer the surface.

HOW DO I FIND THEM?
Run your fingers over your skin, experimenting with soft stroking or circular movements. Alternatively, get your man to do the honors, using his fingers, his tongue, his lips, a feather or even a soft, fluffy makeup brush or paintbrush. The trick is to do it using the lightest of pressures, making your nerve endings tingle with anticipation.

HIT THE SPOT
Set your man a mission—to explore all the hidden, often neglected parts of your body. As well as your wrists, elbows,

and knees, get him to explore the creases underneath your buttocks and breasts, the delicate skin behind your ears, and even your underarms (just make sure you've de-fuzzed first). Who knows, he may just discover a completely new erogenous zone altogether...

IT WORKS FOR ME!
Last year, my boyfriend and I were playing a sexy board game he bought me for Christmas, and as one of the rules, he had to tickle my inner elbows and knees with something soft. I've got some peacock feathers in a vase in my living room, so he used one of those. I thought it sounded a bit stupid, but I soon stopped laughing, as it made my skin tingle in a really sexy way. I confess, we abandoned the board game soon after that, so we could explore other areas with the feather—and we made some very, er, interesting discoveries! Now it's become a regular part of our foreplay.
RACHAEL, 25

THE LIPS

WHAT ARE THEY?
The skin on your lips is the thinnest on your body—made up of just five layers of cells, compared to body skin, which has sixteen. Lips contain a high number of sensitive nerve endings, which lie very close to the surface and are concentrated around your outer lip line; as a result, they're super-sensitive to touch, warmth, and cold. Seen as a sex symbol since time began, it's been suggested men find women's lips particularly attractive because they mimic the appearance of your vaginal lips. In fact, the ancient Indians believed a

woman's upper lip was connected to her clitoris—which might explain why passionate kisses can get you in a saucy mood in seconds.

HOW DO I FIND THEM?

You'll definitely need a partner for this one! Everyone's kissing style is different—and what feels sexy for some people may feel like a vacuum cleaner to others, but don't just stick to safe, straight pecks or French kisses. Mix it up a little, by brushing your lips against your man's; blowing on them; licking them; nibbling them gently; or sucking on them—this draws more blood to your lips, making them feel deliciously tingly.

HIT THE SPOT

Try concentrating on just the top or bottom lip; or kissing after drinking a hot or minty drink; or sucking an ice cube—your lips will love the change in temperature and sensation.

IT WORKS FOR ME!

I'm a huge fan of kissing. There's nothing more exciting than moving in for a kiss with someone you really, really like. Done wrongly, it's horrible, but if you get it just right—not too wet, and with the perfect pressure—then it's the best thing in the world. I couldn't stay with a man who wasn't a great kisser; luckily, my current boyfriend gets five stars. He's as big a kissing addict as I am. If I'm totally honest, given the choice, I might even choose kissing over sex itself!

JENNIFER, 29

THE U SPOT

WHAT IS IT?
A small patch of sensitive tissue on either side of your urethral opening. Experts say, if you caress this area with a moist finger or tongue, you'll enjoy an unexpectedly powerful response.

HOW DO I FIND IT?
The opening of the urethra lies an inch or so below the clitoris and just above the vaginal entrance.

HIT THE SPOT
It's best to make small circles around the U spot with your finger (or your man's tongue), but to avoid probing the area, which could be more than a little uncomfortable. For extra oomph, as you rub the area you can stimulate your clitoris at the same time. Don't worry if you don't experience fireworks, though—the U spot is a very personal thing, which, like G-spot stimulation, you'll either love or hate. But hey, it never hurts to experiment, right?

IT WORKS FOR ME!
I've always been a bit squeamish about my vagina—and didn't think there was anything remotely sexy about my pee hole—until my new boyfriend went down on me for the first time. I was attracted to him like mad, and he seemed to know what he was doing, so when his tongue started circling my urethra, I tensed up a bit at first, but then decided to let him carry on. Once I allowed myself to enjoy it, it felt incredibly sexy (per-

haps the fact it seemed so wrong added a little bit of extra excitement), and that, combined with his excellent technique elsewhere on my genitals, made me come harder than ever before. Now I can't wait for him to explore more previously unchartered territory...

KIM, 25

THE P SPOT

WHAT IS IT?
"P" stands for "perineum"—the official name for the area between your vagina and anus—which is jam-packed with sensitive nerve endings.

HOW DO I FIND IT?
It's a small piece of smooth skin, easily accessible, but often neglected. Oh, and your man has one, too, in the same place—so if he helps you find yours, you can offer to return the favor.

HIT THE SPOT
Ask your man to press your P spot firmly, then let go. If he continues with little pulses like this, in the right place, the effects can be surprisingly pleasing. Alternatively, ask him to press it when you orgasm (or do it yourself during DIY sex)—some women find it makes their orgasms even more powerful.

IT WORKS FOR ME!
I'd heard men love having their perineums stroked or pressed, especially at the point of climax, so I decided to try it on my last boyfriend. He was so surprised, he nearly exploded!

Having seen the effect it had on him, I wanted a piece of the action, too. I asked him to do the same to me the next time I had an orgasm. I could see why he loved it so much—it was incredible! It was like pressing the "bass boost" button on a stereo—everything seemed just a little bit more intense. My boyfriend and I have since split up, but I now practice the technique on my own—using my left finger to press my perineum while I stroke my clitoris with my right. It proves you don't need a man to have a great orgasm!

JILL, 23

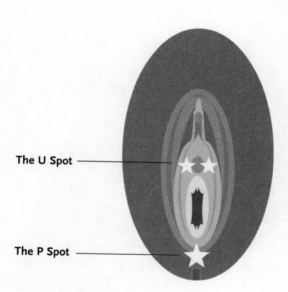

The U Spot

The P Spot

THE A SPOT

WHAT IS IT?

Also known as the slightly less catchy AFE (anterior fornix erotic) zone, this little hot spot is a patch of sensitive tissue at the inner end of the vagina, just above your cervix. Admittedly, it's fairly tricky to find, but putting pressure on the spot is one of the fastest ways to get a super-lubricated vagina (think of it as ten-second foreplay), and direct stimulation can produce violent, orgasmic contractions. As a bonus, unlike the clitoris, it doesn't become oversensitive immediately after an orgasm—so, once you've struck gold, you're in for hours of fun!

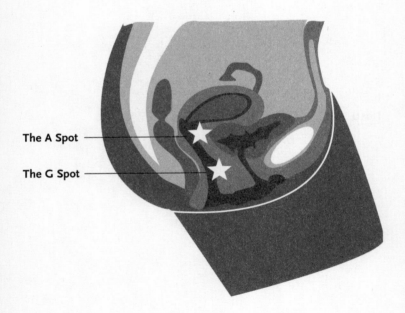

The A Spot

The G Spot

HOW DO I FIND IT?

Feel for a patch of smooth, sensitive tissue at the inner end of your vagina, between your cervix and your bladder.

HIT THE SPOT

You can buy special vibrators, which are long, thin, and upwardly curved at the end, with a bullet-shaped tip—they're usually designed to hit your G spot, but they can also tickle your A spot perfectly, too.

IT WORKS FOR ME!

I read about the A spot on the Internet. My husband and I are quite open about sex, and we love a challenge in bed, so I immediately wanted to see if we could find it. We didn't have much luck using just fingers—either mine or his—as they weren't long enough; but when we tried with a long sex toy called a crystal wand, I definitely felt some strange sensations, and came really quickly. It sounds weird, but knowing we were doing something so experimental—and that I could trust my husband 100 percent with one of the most sensitive parts of my body—was a huge turn-on, so whether we really have found the A spot or not, I'd say it's definitely worth trying!

MEGAN, 31

THE G SPOT

WHAT IS IT?

The most famous erogenous zone of them all, the G spot was given its name by scientist Ernst Gräfenberg in the 1950s. It's a small mass of flat, smooth tissue located inside the vagina, about a third of the way up the front wall—closest to your stomach. Some sexperts still argue it doesn't exist, and Gräfenberg was barking up the wrong tree, as not every woman enjoys having this area stimulated—but G-spot devotees say it produces a wide wave of pleasure when you climax, as opposed to the more intense feel of a clitoral orgasm. Some women even ejaculate a clear liquid during a G-spot orgasm—don't worry, it's not pee, it's just vaginal fluid, and means you're a very lucky lady indeed.

HOW DO I FIND IT?

Locating it yourself can be difficult, so the best way is to enlist the help of your man. Get him to use his index or middle finger (with his palm facing him) and push softly on the lower third of the vagina's front wall until he finds a sensitive place—a small, almond-shaped patch that feels different to the surrounding skin. He should then move his finger in small circles, or pulse it lightly on the spot. If you're alone and having problems finding it, try pressing a little harder than you would on your clitoris; placing a flat hand on your pubic mound and gently pushing down at the same time; or search for it after an orgasm, when the area has swelled slightly.

HIT THE SPOT

You can stimulate your G spot either through intercourse or manually, using your fingers or a special curved vibrator or dildo. If your man is using his hand, lie down and put pillows underneath your bottom to make it easier for him. To reach the G spot during sex, opt for positions where you're on top, or he enters from behind.

IT WORKS FOR ME!

I'd searched for my G spot with past partners, but had no joy until my current boyfriend gave me my first G-spot orgasm last year, at the age of twenty-eight. I have to be fully aroused, so we'll spend about half an hour on foreplay—then he gently inserts his fingers in my vagina and moves them in a repetitive beckoning motion. Once he gets into his rhythm, I come within minutes. It's a different feeling to a clitoral orgasm—my whole body seems to pulse and it's incredibly intense. I really have to be in the mood, though, so it's not something we do every time we have sex—we save it for special occasions!

OLIVIA, 29

G-SPOT SURGERY

Cosmetic surgeons are forever dreaming up new ways to improve or enhance what nature gave us, and now a new operation to enhance your sex life has been unveiled. It involves injecting fillers, such as collagen—usually used to plump up lips—into your G spot. Apparently, the filler boosts sensitivity and so it's easier to, er, hit the spot during sex. But before you hand over your hard-earned cash, it's worth considering that not everyone gets pleasure out of having their love button plumped up. And if you have an allergic reaction, it'll be painful beyond belief. If you're determined to go ahead, though, be sure you're okay with letting a male surgeon get up close and personal with your G spot—most men have trouble finding it, let alone sticking a needle in it!

I HAD MY G SPOT ENHANCED

Sally, 30, asked her cosmetic surgeon to give her a helping hand in the bedroom.

I'm a Botox fan, and I love trying out nonsurgical beauty treatments, so the surgeon at my local clinic offered me a discount to try a treatment which increases the sensitivity of your G spot by injecting it with hyaluronic acid, a filler usually used to plump up lips. I had a boyfriend, and my sex life was okay, but not as good as I thought it could be, so I decided to give it a go.

I was unlikely to have an allergic reaction to the filler, as I'd had it injected in my lips in the past. I was warned that the procedure is only temporary—the effects wear off after three to four months, and 10 percent of women feel no benefit at all.

The injection itself was like having a pap smear. The surgeon put some local anesthetic cream in my vagina, and then I lay down on a couch as he inserted a clamp like the ones used in Pap smear tests. Once the surgeon had located the right area (apparently your G spot has a different surface to the rest of your skin—it's rough, like orange peel), he injected it with two syringes of filler. It took twenty minutes—there was a burning sensation for a while, and I was a bit sore where the needle had gone in, but after half an hour I felt normal.

My boyfriend and I waited a couple of days to have sex, and when we did, I noticed the difference—my orgasms improved instantly. My female friends were all eager to try it; in fact, one of them already has. The effects have worn off now, and my sex life is back to how it was before. It's not cheap, so I'd only do it again as a special treat, with a surgeon I trust, as it's such a sensitive area.

Chapter 6
TAKE YOUR POSITIONS

MY BEST EVER ORGASM...
I used to have a boyfriend whose penis was slightly bent to one side when it was erect. I'm not sure exactly where he was pressing inside me, but in certain positions, it felt amazing— definitely better than a straight one! The orgasms he gave me took my breath away.
   CHARLOTTE, 29

ON YOUR MARKS, GET SET...

You shouldn't have to be a gymnast with arms of steel and superhuman stamina to have great sex. Yet books like the Kama Sutra are full of poses that look more like complicated, advanced yoga postures than sexual positions. Perhaps that's why so many couples stick to a few tried-and-trusted favorites, like missionary or doggie style.

Yet while these can be very effective, they don't always hit the right spots, or produce the desired end result—an orgasm for you. That's why I've whittled down the thousands of sexual positions out there to just ten. Forget uncomfortable, impossible contortions—these positions are all guaranteed to be easy, satisfying and produce surprisingly orgasmic results. To prove it, I asked two couples—one in the take-me-now throes of a new relationship, and one longer-term pair who know each other intimately—to try them all out...

THE TESTERS:

THE NEW COUPLE:
Rachel, 23, and Bradley, 25, have been together for two months. They describe their bedroom style as: "Passionate and experimental."

THE LONG-TERM COUPLE:
Josh, 34, and Lily, 28, have been together for two years. They describe their bedroom style as: "Frequent, varied, and adventurous!"

THE POSITIONS:

THE CROUCHING TIGER

ASSUME THE POSITION:
Kneel on all fours, as you would in the doggie-style position. Then, bend at your waist, until you're leaning on your forearms, and your head is touching the bed. Your man then kneels at your feet, and enters you from behind.

WHAT'S IN IT FOR YOU?
Much more comfortable than doggie style, you get to concentrate on the satisfyingly deep penetration without "Ouch-

my-arms-are-going-to-give-way" muscle fatigue spoiling your enjoyment.

WHAT'S IN IT FOR HIM?

As you're supporting yourself, your man can thrust away happily—plus, his hands are free to explore wherever he pleases.

ADVANCED MOVES:

As you're so stable, get him to use one of his hands to reach around and play with your clitoris, for extra va-va-voom factor!

TESTERS' VERDICTS

Rachel: "This position felt amazing—and very naughty—especially as there was pretty much nothing I could do, and Bradley was in full control. He was able to get deep inside me, and thrust hard, which gave me a really intense orgasm."

Bradley: "Incredible! It felt really dirty—much deeper than usual doggie style, and it definitely seemed to hit the right spot for Rachel. This was a very sexy experience, with a fantastic ending which left both of us craving an encore. We'll be trying it at every opportunity from now on."

Lily: "This position is a change from the normal doggie style, and the deeper penetration does work. It allowed Josh to be more 'hands free' than usual, because I could rest my weight totally on my shoulders."

Josh: "This position pleasantly surprised me, as it was fantastic! Although doggie is already one of my favorites, this was different—it felt much tighter, and I could see that not having to hold Lily's body steady meant she enjoyed it more than usual. Out of all the positions we tried, this was the best one for me, as my orgasm was the most intense."

THE SCISSORS

ASSUME THE POSITION:

Get into the missionary position, with your man on top. He enters you, then pivots slightly, so although your pelvises are still locked together, his head and upper body fall to one side of yours, while one of his legs now lies between your legs, and the other lies outside. From above, you'll look very much like a pair of open scissors.

WHAT'S IN IT FOR YOU?

The downward pressure on your pubic area and clitoris creates a delicious friction. If you prefer slow-burn sex to quickies, you'll love this position, as it works by building up pressure steadily.

WHAT'S IN IT FOR HIM?

The change of angle, together with the pressure on his pubic area, should pleasantly surprise him!

ADVANCED MOVES:

Rise your pelvis up to meet his as he thrusts, for even more friction—and explosive results.

TESTERS' VERDICTS

Rachel: "This was simple yet pleasurable. The slightly different angle at which Bradley entered me gave me different sensations to missionary and, as I felt really relaxed, my orgasm was much stronger."

Bradley: "I was more than pleasantly surprised by this. Although I wasn't as deep as usual, the change in angle, and the fact she could run her hands all over me, gave explosive results."

Lily: "I absolutely loved this. Josh was able to rub me in exactly the right spot, and gave me a really powerful orgasm. The fact we had to move slowly together built up more friction."

Josh: "It was a strange position to lie in, as it felt a bit methodical. There's definitely more in it for the ladies, though, as it rubbed Lily in all the right places."

THE SEE-SAW

ASSUME THE POSITION:

Your man lies on his back. You then kneel over his pelvis, with your legs either side of his body, and your shins resting on the bed. Next, lower yourself on to his penis, and place your palms on his lower abdomen. This is your starting position. However, rather than bouncing up and down, you then lean forward slightly, sliding yourself up his penis, until you're resting your palms on his upper chest, and your forearms are almost touching it. Next, slowly lean back, moving down his penis as you do so, and return to the starting position. Repeat, until you've built up a rhythm.

WHAT'S IN IT FOR YOU?

As you lean forward, your clitoris rubs along his body; and as you sit back up, his helmet brushes against your G spot. Oh, and you're in complete control, meaning orgasm is 100 percent more likely.

WHAT'S IN IT FOR HIM?

He gets to lie there while his penis is treated to a fantastic sliding sensation. What more could a man want?

ADVANCED MOVES:

Try squeezing your pelvic floor muscles (the ones you'd tighten when trying to stop peeing midstream) as you work your way up and down his penis. It'll fast-forward your orgasm—and he'll be in heaven!

TESTERS' VERDICTS

Rachel: "Once I got into a rhythm, I loved this position. Being in control, and being able to squeeze my pelvic floor muscles, kiss, and keep eye contact with Bradley while he caressed my boobs, gave us both an incredible climax."

Bradley: "I felt completely dominated throughout—there wasn't much I could do, so I just lay back and enjoyed the show! I had an awesome view, and once Rachel hit her rhythm, I could tell it was hitting all the right buttons at the right time."

Lily: "We found this the most difficult, as it took a few goes for us to get the most out of it. But after a few attempts, we got the hang of it—Josh enjoyed me being in charge, and it meant I could be totally in control."

Josh: "I liked Lily being on top and in control—and once she'd mastered the rocking maneuver, I could feel her rubbing along the shaft of my penis, which was nice. My orgasm was okay, although not mind-blowing."

THE SPACE HOPPER

ASSUME THE POSITION:
Your man lies on his back. You then squat over his penis, facing him, in a crouching position, with your feet on either side of his thighs. Rest your hands on his ribcage for support, then, using your thighs as leverage, bounce gently up and down on his penis.

WHAT'S IN IT FOR YOU?
You're in charge of the depth of penetration, and can set the pace, speeding up or slowing down when you want it most.

WHAT'S IN IT FOR HIM?

He gets to watch your body jiggling around above him—trust me, he won't complain!

ADVANCED MOVES:

Rather than moving straight up and down his penis, try pulsing at the top for a few beats, to buildup the tension, before plunging back down again. The downward slide will feel twice as pleasurable.

TESTERS' VERDICTS

Rachel: "This wasn't particularly comfortable, and I had to cheat and sink down on to my shins to make it work!"

Bradley: "This was more of a giggle than being sexy. I could tell it wasn't particularly comfortable for Rachel, but we both got into the spirit of it and had a laugh, which is always a good thing to do in bed."

Lily: "My God, this was great exercise! Being able to sustain the bouncing was quite hard, but very amusing. I was able to be in control again, and could get as much penetration as I wanted."

Josh: "I remember the original space hoppers, and this position is aptly named! I really enjoyed her doing all the work."

THE CAT (COITAL ALIGNMENT TECHNIQUE)

ASSUME THE POSITION:

Get into the missionary position, with your man on top. Once he's entered you, he shifts his body further up yours, so your

two pelvises align. He'll find only the head of his penis remains inside you. You then wrap your legs around his, so your ankles are about the same height as his calves. During sex, forget thrusting—you both move your pelvises away from each other and then together again, in a subtle, yet powerful, rocking motion.

WHAT'S IN IT FOR YOU?

The CAT is great for stimulating your clitoris during sex, so orgasm is practically guaranteed. The shallow angle also means your man is more likely to hit your G spot, so the odds of a penetrative orgasm are raised, too. Add to this the fact you get maximum body contact, as well as being able to kiss at the same time, and it's probably as near perfect a position as you can get!

WHAT'S IN IT FOR HIM?
The ultrasensitive head of his penis gets lavished with attention; plus, once you've climaxed, he can thrust in and out until he comes too.

ADVANCED MOVES:
If you're feeling generous, give him a treat by clenching your pelvic floor muscles to grip his penis as he moves inside you.

TESTERS' VERDICTS
Rachel: "A really teasing position with full body contact, which got us both aroused very quickly. We couldn't help but get carried away with this one—things got intense and passionate within minutes, leading to a very sensual orgasm."

Bradley: "It was slightly confusing getting into position, and when you're in the mood, instructions tend to fall by the wayside. But judging by the end result, I think we cracked it!"

Lily: "This was my favorite! It rubbed much more on my clitoris than any other position, and brought me to orgasm quicker than usual. We could kiss passionately during it, and I managed to clench my pelvic floor, which was a massive turn-on for Josh."

Josh: "This was in my top three. I felt really close to Lily, and could kiss her and canoodle with her, while all the time knowing my hips were rubbing her in the right places and driving her wild. Rubbing hips can be a little uncomfortable, but you soon forget about it—particularly when Lily was enjoying it so much she started making some fantastic noises. Incredible!"

SPOONS

ASSUME THE POSITION:
Lie on your side. Your man lies on his side behind you, and enters you from behind.

WHAT'S IN IT FOR YOU?
If you're after a lazy Sunday morning lie-in position, find deep thrusting uncomfortable, or if you're pregnant and your bump tends to get in the way during sex—this is for you. The angle of entry means the first few inches of your vagina—the bit with the most nerve endings—gets stimulated, along with your G spot. And all this without you having to do much work at all!

WHAT'S IN IT FOR HIM?
His hands are free to explore your body and boobs to his heart's content. Oh, and apparently the sight of a woman's buttocks brings out primal urges in men. Which can only be a good thing.

ADVANCED MOVES:
Want him to go deeper? Bend at the waist slightly, moving your upper body away from your man, for increased pene-

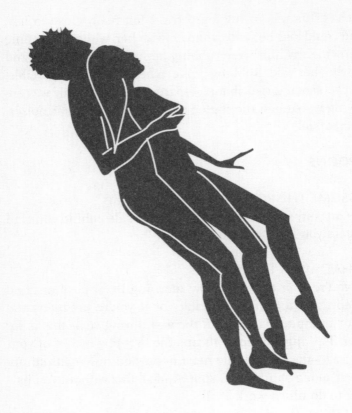

tration. Need a little help reaching the big O? Get him to put his free hand to good use, by playing with your clitoris at the same time as he thrusts.

TESTERS' VERDICTS
Rachel: "This was my favorite position, as it made for really erotic sex. I loved the feeling of being 'taken,' as he thrust deeper. My G spot was stimulated, and Bradley could use

his free hand to play with my clitoris. I had an orgasm every time we tried it!"

Bradley: "This is by far the most intimate position ever. I could kiss and touch Rachel everywhere. Because of the angle, and the fact I decided I wanted to see her face, it led to numerous other positions I don't even think have names! All in all, for me, this is as good as it gets."

"To perform this position well, I think you have to be roughly the same size—it doesn't help if, like me and Josh, one of you is 5'4", while the other is over 6'! However, we tweaked it a little—Josh leaned forward slightly—and it worked great. It's a great lazy sex position—I like positions that make Josh's penis rub the entrance to my vagina, so this was perfect."

Josh: "This is something you can both enjoy without needing major bedroom gymnastics; and like the CAT, you get to feel close to each other. It wasn't particularly orgasmic for me, but I loved being able to put my arms around Lily, and turn her on with my hands at the same time as thrusting."

THE TWISTER

ASSUME THE POSITION:
You and your man both lie on your sides, facing each other, with the fronts of your thighs touching, and your arms around each other's bodies. You then lift your top leg, bend it towards your chest—so it forms a right angle with your body—and then rest it over his top thigh. He then bends his top thigh underneath yours.

WHAT'S IN IT FOR YOU?

The gentle rocking motion needed in this position ensures the sensitive nerve endings in your inner thighs get plenty of attention.

WHAT'S IN IT FOR HIM?

As well as being able to caress your butt, he gets to look you straight in the eye during sex—a huge turn-on.

ADVANCED MOVES:

Want to speed things up a little? Get your man to slip on a vibrating cock ring just before he enters you (see chapter seven, page 106). He'll love the tingling sensation, while you'll love the way it turns his penis into a real-life vibrator!

TESTERS' VERDICTS

Rachel: "The slow, unhurried penetration meant I got aroused slowly—building with the rhythm of thrusting. All in all, I found it a very sensitive, passionate, and surprisingly easy position, which gave a more controlled orgasm than usual."

Bradley: "This was very intimate, as I could feel all of Rachel's body pressing against mine. Although it was a little uncomfortable at times, I loved having her legs wrapped around me, and as it felt so tight, I could tell every time I hit the right spot. I had a very passionate, and sexy, orgasm."

Lily: "This position is intimate from the beginning, as you lie facing each other. You can take as long as you need turning each other on—kissing and stroking—before slowly maneuvering your legs into position. Josh's pelvis rubbed on my clitoris, meaning my orgasm came on slowly, and was more intense when it finally arrived."

Josh: "I liked the intimacy, but I didn't really get much out of this orgasm-wise—I was concentrating on being in the right position too much—but I was obviously doing something right, as I could tell Lily loved it."

THE REVERSE MISSIONARY

ASSUME THE POSITION:

Get into the missionary position—but this time, you're on top. Your man should lie beneath you, with his legs straight, and his arms flat by his sides. Allow him to enter you, then lie exactly on top of him, with your legs straight, mirroring his. Next, place your hands on either side of his upper arms, and use them to shuffle your body slowly up and down his, while keeping your thighs clamped together for extra friction.

WHAT'S IN IT FOR YOU?
Again, you get to set the pace, and as you slide up and down, his pubic bone grazes your clitoris.

WHAT'S IN IT FOR HIM?
The knowledge that he's hitting all the right spots without having to make much effort.

ADVANCED MOVES:
Having problems? Get more leverage by asking your man to move his legs apart slightly, so you can rest both your legs between his.

TESTERS' VERDICTS
Rachel: "This position tightened vaginal entry, and being in control increased the friction. Bradley rubbing my clitoris with his pubic bone, together with moving my hips in circles, led to a fantastic orgasm."

Bradley: "I didn't feel very manly in this position, but to be fair, it was nice to feel Rachel lying on top of me. It made for a very intense experience, but I never felt like I was deep enough, so it's not something I'll be initiating often."

Lily: "Another position where I was in control. There wasn't much movement, which meant Josh rubbed perfectly on my clitoris. We could kiss hard, and Josh could grab my butt. I didn't orgasm purely from this position—but it did bring me further than halfway."

Josh: "I liked the focus on rubbing all the right places, and enjoyed being able to kiss Lily at the same time. However, penetration wasn't as deep, so it wasn't as enjoyable for me as other positions."

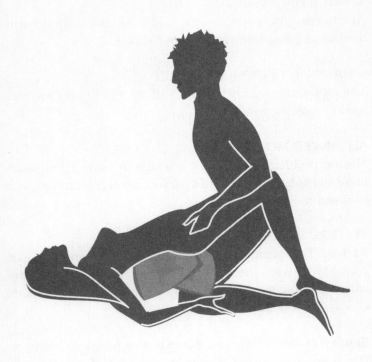

THE PELVIC LIFT

ASSUME THE POSITION:
Your man kneels up, so his shins are touching the bed. You lie on your back, facing him, and place a couple of pillows under your bottom, to raise your pelvis upwards. Next, put your legs on either side of your man's body, bend your knees, and rest your feet flat on the bed. He then enters you, and grasps hold of your bottom, pulling you towards him.

WHAT'S IN IT FOR YOU?
You get deep penetration with added comfort, thanks to the pillows. The angle also means his penis rubs against your G spot.

WHAT'S IN IT FOR HIM?
Unlike most positions, he gets to watch his penis as it enters and withdraws from you—sex doesn't get much more satisfying than this.

ADVANCED MOVES:
Ensure he hits all the right spots by moving your pelvis in a circular motion while he thrusts.

TESTERS' VERDICTS
Rachel: "Bradley could get really deep inside me, but it felt good having more control, as I could guide him when I wanted him to go harder. The pillows definitely made this position easier, and more comfortable, allowing us both to enjoy the ride."

Bradley: "I liked this one a lot, as I could see Rachel's expression throughout. I seemed to be getting a good reaction, and it felt really deep. This position made it easier for me to be a bit rougher than usual, which, needless to say, I loved!"

Lily: "Another favorite of mine. Having the pillow under my butt made for really deep penetration. I could touch myself in this position, and we could make it faster or slower, depending on whether just one of us was moving, or we both moved together. My orgasm was slow, yet powerful."

Josh: "I really liked this position. The pillow allows for a different angle of penetration to usual, and it rubbed me in all the right places. I could also feel Lily getting really turned on—and that's always a bonus."

THE BACKWARDS FROG

ASSUME THE POSITION:
Your man kneels up, so his shins are flat on the bed. You lie on your back, facing him. He then lifts your legs up, until the backs of your thighs are resting on his chest, and his head is between your calves. He then enters you, and leans forward, bringing the fronts of your thighs towards your boobs, until he's resting his hands on the bed on either side of your body, for support.

WHAT'S IN IT FOR YOU?
The ultimate in G-spot stimulation and deep penetration, you'll feel his penis further inside you than you ever thought possible. If you press a hand to your lower stomach, you can even feel him moving inside.

WHAT'S IN IT FOR HIM?
He'll love the deep penetration and the fact he's in control here (well, it's only fair to let him in on the fun).

ADVANCED MOVES:
He can vary the depth of penetration by leaning further forwards or backwards; while you can change the sensation by moving your legs to one side, or opening them further and hooking your knees over his elbows.

TESTERS' VERDICTS

Rachel: "The pressure of Bradley's penis thrusting deep inside me felt great, and meant the buildup to orgasm was really intense. The eye contact made it really intimate, as I saw how much he was enjoying it too."

Bradley: "I was totally in control throughout, which was great. It gave me an incredible opportunity to appreciate her legs and body, while getting seriously deep. I particularly loved it when she tightened her legs around my neck as she climaxed—maybe she was more in control than I originally thought!"

Lily: "By far one of the best positions. I loved the deep penetration this gave, and that Josh was able to vary his depth by moving in further, or teasing me by half pulling out. We tried it with my legs over his shoulders, and also pulling my knees to my chest, which allowed Josh to kiss me while playing with my clitoris and breasts. When it came, my orgasm was worth waiting for."

Josh: "I loved this. It was quite hard work, but fun, too. I loved going really deep, and it rubbed the end of my penis, which made my orgasm really intense."

Chapter 7
DIY ORGASMS

MY BEST EVER ORGASM...
I've got to say some of my best orgasms are ones I've given myself, as there's no pressure to please anybody else. It's taken me years of practice, and it's been frustrating at times, but now I've worked out exactly what works and what doesn't. Now I can give myself an orgasm any time I want. It's improved the orgasms I have with my boyfriend, too—now I know what turns me on, I can let him in on the secret!
JANE, 30

MASTURBATION—THE BEST FUN YOU CAN HAVE ON YOUR OWN

As the saying goes, if you want a job done properly, do it yourself. And when it comes to orgasms, that's certainly true. The thing is, while sexual positions, the size of his penis, and even sex toys are all regular discussion topics for a girls' night out, mention the word "masturbation" and you'll be met with an awkward silence. Solo sex is still a bit of a taboo subject, partly because of the myth it's something you only do if you're not getting it regularly! However, sexperts reckon over 80 percent of women regularly indulge in a little DIY down below; and when *Company* magazine asked its readers to spill the beans on their masturbation habits, only 25 percent said they did it less than once a month—whereas a very happy 10 percent claimed to have a self-pleasing session three times a week or more.

Many women have their first orgasm through masturbation, and some even prefer it to full-on sex. So, even if you think you're not a fan, maybe it's worth giving it another go. Besides, if you don't know what turns you on, how on earth can you expect a man to? In case you're not doing it yet, or want to perfect your technique, here's a masturbation master class, just for you.

THE BEGINNER'S GUIDE TO THE BASICS

ON YOUR MARKS...

The first rule of solo sex is atmosphere. The last thing you want is a phone call from your mom just as you're reaching the point of no return. Switch off your cell, lock the door, and draw the curtains—you'll instantly feel more relaxed. Some women like to light a scented candle, dim the lights, or even put on some soothing music, but you should do whatever's right for you.

GET SET...

The most popular position is on your back in bed, although some women prefer to do it sitting cross-legged with their backs against the wall; standing in front of a mirror, so they can watch themselves; or in a warm bath. If you're a missionary masturbator, occasionally try another way, like lying on your stomach, or kneeling—you may get different results. You might also want to make sure you've got a tube of lubricant handy. Next, get your juices flowing by giving yourself a sexy massage with moisturizer, massage oil, or baby oil. Take a small amount in your palm and run your hands over your neck, breasts, arms, inner thighs, and stomach, but steer clear of your clitoris for the time being. Try alternating feather-light touches and gentle pressure, noticing as you do so which feels best. You may find it helps to read some erotic fiction, watch a favorite movie sex scene, or fantasize about Johnny Depp while doing this.

GO!

Once you're feeling turned on (and there's no rush—this could take any length of time, depending on what Johnny's doing to you in your head), slowly let your hand wander down towards your genitals. Run your fingers around the outer lips of your vagina and over the whole area, rubbing, stroking, and pressing softly until you find the type of touch that feels best. When you're ready, take one finger and either lick it or add a small blob of lubricant, to help things go more smoothly. Slowly circle the outside of your clitoris with your finger, applying a subtle pressure and keeping up a steady rhythm. As you become more practiced, you could try up-and-down movements, or even stroke the clitoris itself, if it's not too sensitive. Not sure where your clitoris is? Take a mirror and look for the small bump hidden in the lips at the top of your vaginal opening.

After a while (and this really could be anything from five to fifty minutes), the feelings down below should begin to buildup—you may want to speed things up or press slightly harder at this point. But try not to get too obsessed about having an orgasm the very first time you masturbate—just relax and try to enjoy the different sensations. If and when you do eventually reach the big O, don't worry—you'll know about it.

ADVANCED TECHNIQUES

Once you've grasped the basics, it's time to branch out and experiment. There are literally hundreds of different ways you can get your rocks off—it's just a matter of finding the methods that work for you.

IN WATER

Some women like to masturbate in the bath or shower, using soapy hands, a running tap, or the stream from a shower-head to reach orgasm. The consistent flow of warm water on your vagina can feel amazing. A few words of advice here, though: try to avoid putting soapy fingers up your vagina—it's very drying and could bring on a bout of candida (definitely not sexy). If you're using a shower attachment or a tap, make sure the stream runs across your vagina, rather than straight up it, for the same reason.

USING FRICTION

Rather than using your fingers, try rubbing your vagina against something else instead. Moving up and down against a cushion, pillow, mattress, chair, or bench works for some women, while others prefer to rub the end of a duvet, the seam of their jeans, or even a soft toy between their legs. Experiment with as many different textures as possible—you'll soon realize when you've picked a winner.

WITH LUBRICANTS

You might think you get wet enough already during a masturbation session, but a dollop of lubricant can literally transform your solo sex life. Water-based varieties are great as they don't stain sheets and, unlike oil-based ones, are safe to use with latex sex toys; while silicone-based varieties feel silky smooth and can be used underwater. Want to experiment further? Minty lubes will make your vagina feel deliciously cool and tingly. Other specially created formulas will make it feel warm—and they'll heat up even further when you rub or blow on them.

WITH YOUR THIGHS

Some women claim they can teach themselves to reach orgasm by simply pushing their thighs together. If you want to try it, start by masturbating as you would usually, then squeeze your thighs together when you climax. Practice this regularly, and after a few weeks, pull your fingers away just before orgasm, and then try to tip yourself over the edge by squeezing your thighs. Once you've mastered this, start the thigh-squeezing moves sooner each time you masturbate—eventually, fans of this technique claim, you'll hardly need to use your fingers first at all before you come. Now that's a skill worth learning!

MASTURBATION CHANGED MY LIFE

Laura, 26, faked her orgasms for five years until she learned how to masturbate.

I first had sex when I was twenty. My boyfriend was very experienced. While he made me feel comfortable and sexy in bed, he couldn't make me climax. Naively, I assumed I must be the one with the problem, so I'm ashamed to say, I began faking my orgasms.

When my boyfriend and I split up a year later, I threw myself into a round of one-night stands. I thought mind-blowing sex was just a matter of finding the right man. But the only thing I got out of it was a bad case of candida.

Then, about three years ago, I started going out with Ross. We were work colleagues at first, but one evening, we decided to take things a step further. I didn't have an orgasm that night, but I came closer to it than ever before.

Ross and I started seeing each other regularly. I thought he wouldn't like me if he knew about my orgasm problem, so I continued to fake it, which made me feel incredibly guilty, especially as the rest of our relationship was going so well.

I knew something had to change, but I didn't want to tell Ross I'd been lying, so I tried to sort out my problem on my own. I began researching on the Internet and found out I had what's known as anorgasmia—the inability to reach orgasm. Luckily, the condition can be temporary, and a lot of the barriers are mental, not physical.

Three months into the relationship, I was flicking through a magazine when I found a feature on masturbation. I'd tried it a few times before and never had much luck—to be honest, I found the whole idea a bit seedy—but I was desperate, and decided to give it another go. I waited until my roommates were out, and drew the curtains. I followed the instructions in the article to the letter, and I began to get feelings I'd never experienced before. I didn't manage to come that first time, but I kept trying, and a few nights later, I finally had an orgasm. My first feeling was of immense relief—I was normal!

After that, I practiced giving myself orgasms, until eventually I knew exactly what pressure and movements I needed. Then, one night in bed with Ross, I directed his hands down *below and told him how I wanted him to touch me. When I came, I started crying—I knew I'd found the man for me.*

I still haven't had an orgasm through penetration alone, but as long as I get some manual stimulation, I can come. Ross and I now have a fantastic sex life—in fact, we recently had a baby, so we must be doing something right! If anyone reading this is nervous about having a go at solo sex, don't knock it until you've tried it. I can honestly say masturbation has changed my life. Give it a try tonight.

SEX TOYS—THE ULTIMATE SOLO SEX ACCESSORIES

With female-friendly sex shops, designer sex aids, and even British film comedies about vibrators (Rabbit Fever, 2006), sex toys have hit the mainstream. In fact, a 2006 survey by condom makers Durex found 43 percent of people in Britain own a vibrator. With US sex retailer Good Vibrations now raking in 12.5 million a year alone, for some women, going shopping for sex toys is as easy—and as fun—as buying a new pair of heels. If you haven't joined them yet, isn't it time you got a flexible friend of your own?

With thousands of different types, shapes, lengths, and materials to choose from, buying your first toy can be incredibly daunting. To help you narrow down the selection, first ask yourself what kind of stimulation you like during sex—do you like the feeling of fullness during penetration? (In which case, a dildo, bullet, or love egg might be ideal.) Or does clitoral stimulation do it for you? (You might prefer a vibrator or clitoral stimulator.) Do you do it in the bath (then go for a waterproof toy), or when you're away (try a bullet or clitoral stimulator)? If you're still unsure, read on...

VIBRATORS

Vibrators do exactly what it says on the package—small motors inside drive mini-rotating weights, causing the whole thing to vibrate. The buzzing feels so good because it increases the blood flow to your vagina, making it super-sensitive. You can hold vibes against your clitoris, or use the longer ones for penetration. Most work using batteries, or can be charged up, like a cell phone; many come with variable speed settings, and the harder the material they're made of (anything from silky silicone to plastic), the stronger the vibrations will be. Gone are the days when vibrators had to look like penises—you can still get incredibly realistic models, complete with veins (lovely!), but there are also ergonomically shaped designer vibes, pocked-sized pleasers, smooth shafts, and even designs specially invented to hit your G spot.

Tip-you-over-the-edge tip: If you find the buzzing too intense, wrap your vibrator in a towel, muffle it with a pillow, or hold it over your hand or finger, to soften and transfer the vibrations.

DILDOS

Often confused with vibrators, dildos are usually longer and slightly narrower than vibrators, and have no moving parts. They're designed for penetration, although you might also like to try rubbing them across your vagina and clitoris with a dollop of lubrication. They're available in practically every material under the sun, from metal and

SPOTLIGHT ON: THE RABBIT

Since its starring role in *Sex and the City*, the Rabbit vibrator has become the best-selling vibrator in the world. In the UK alone, of the 2.5 million sex toys sold by popular sex retailer Ann Summers stores every year, a whopping one million are their trademarked Rampant Rabbits. So, what makes it so special? Apart from the moving head and the knobbly beads, which hit the most sensitive first few inches of your vagina, its secret weapon is the extra, bunny-shaped arm, whose ears are perfectly placed to hit your clitoris. It's now possible to buy a whole family of Rabbits, from waterproof and keyring-sized bunnies, to a techno Rabbit you can control via the Internet!

glass, to jade, plastic, latex, rubber, and silicone, which absorbs body heat and can feel like the real thing. You can opt for a lifelike, penis-shaped model, or a smooth, stiff, or bendy pole. There are even ones with a curvy end, to help reach your G spot. Just like penises, they come in a wide range of lengths and widths, from the super-slim to the monster-sized. If you're unsure which width works for you, hit the vegetable aisle in the supermarket, and buy carrots, cucumbers, and zucchinis of varying sizes. Wash them, then slip on a condom and experiment until you've found the perfect fit!

Tip-you-over-the-edge tip: Feeling experimental? Go for the double whammy by popping a dildo inside you, while using a vibrator on your clitoris.

CLITORAL STIMULATORS

These are mini-vibrators, for external use only, designed especially to hit your C spot. Some come with plastic straps, so you can wear them like panties for hands-free fun, while others fit on to your finger, hang from your keyring, or are shaped like little lipsticks or nail varnishes, for the ultimate in discretion.

Tip-you-over-the-edge tip: Clitoral stimulators tend to be smaller and quieter than full-size vibrators, so they're ideal for traveling. Slip one in your suitcase!

BULLETS

These small, rounded, vibrating bullets can be placed on your genitals, or inserted just inside your vagina (but check they're designed for internal use first). They're either attached by a wire to a control box, or operated by remote control—which can work up to a staggering 50 feet away. The newest bullets plug into your MP3 player and stimulate you in time with your favorite tunes; while others are triggered by your cell phone—they vibrate for twenty seconds when you get a text, or buzz away down below for the duration of your phone call!

Tip-you-over-the-edge tip: Because they're so discreet, bullets are an ideal size for popping in between you and your man's genitals during sex. The subtle vibrations will drive you both wild.

WATERPROOF TOYS

Want a bit of underwater love? While ordinary vibrators can't be used in or near water (the results can be, quite literally, shocking), there are a host of sex toys specially designed for use in the bath, shower, or hot tub. Choose from traditional long or penis-like models, giant vibrating sponges, or opt for something more interesting, like fish, ducks, penguins, hippos, and dolphins, which have all manner of interesting fins, ears, and beaks to place on your genitals. The ducks look so innocent, yours can sit on the edge of the bath and no one will ever suspect he has a naughty double life!

Tip-you-over-the-edge tip: Your natural lubrication can get washed away in all that water, so to help things go more swimmingly, apply a blob of silicone-based water-resistant lubricant to your toy or vagina before you dive in.

LOVE BALLS

Also known as Ben Wa balls, Burmese bells, orgasm balls, or love eggs, these consist of two plastic, latex, or rubber spheres on a cord, which you insert into your vagina. Inside are small metal weights, which jiggle around saucily when you move. While some women find the stimulation they provide is too subtle to notice, others love the delicate wobbles deep in their vagina, and particularly enjoy the fact they can wear them all day without their coworkers or friends being any the wiser! Love balls can also help you to exercise your PC muscles down below (see chapter nine). Simply insert the balls, then squeeze and release your muscles around them, several times a day.

Tip-you-over-the-edge tip: Try inserting the balls before you begin masturbating, then just as you reach orgasm, gently pull them out with the cord—some women claim the sensation of fullness they provide, plus the pop-popping feeling when they're removed, makes their orgasms even stronger.

LETTING YOUR MAN IN ON THE FUN

You might prefer to keep your vibrator to yourself—or, having discovered the joy of sex toys, you may want to share yours with your man. You can use it while he watches, use it on him, or let him take control and use it on you. You could also wedge it between the two of you during sex, or even use it to rub your clitoris while he's inside you. Alternatively, there are hundreds of sex toys created especially for couples—from vibrating cock rings that give you both a buzz, to mini-vibes he can strap on to his tongue when he goes down on you. One word of warning, though: the male ego is a fragile thing, and many men are wary of their vibrating rivals. They wonder why you'd want a synthetic penis when you can have the real thing. So, make sure he understands you're not trying to replace him, or criticize a lackluster performance—you're simply trying something new, and you'd love him to join in the fun. And if he still complains? It's now possible to buy mold-your-own vibrator kits. He makes a buzzing, silicone replica of his equipment, which you can use when he's not around. Perfect!

TLC FOR YOUR TOYS

THE TEN TOY COMMANDMENTS

1. Never share sex toys. If you want to bring someone else in on the fun, pop a condom on your vibrator or dildo first.

2. Don't move a toy from your anus to your vagina without cleaning it first, to avoid infection (or use a fresh condom).

3. Never use toys on cut, swollen, or inflamed skin—they'll only irritate you further, and could cause infection.

4. Inspect all new toys for cracks and hard edges before you play with them. If in doubt, don't use them.

5. Never use a toy for something it wasn't designed for—if it says "not for internal use" on the packaging, there's a good reason why.

6. Don't use a toy in water unless it's specifically labeled as being waterproof—you might get an electric shock.

7. Always clean your toy before and after you use it (see "TLC for Your Toys" on page 108).

8. If you develop a rash or itching down below when using a sex toy, stop. You might be allergic to the material it's made of.

9. Make your toy last longer by removing the batteries when you clean and store it.

10. Moisture, sunlight, and heat can all damage sex toys, so keep yours in a cool, dark place—a laundry bag or shoebox is ideal.

Just as you wouldn't want your man to come near you if he hadn't had a shower since you last had sex, your sex toy should be ultra-clean at all times, too. But before you get the bleach out, different materials require different cleansers. Here's the lowdown.

SILICONE
The easiest substance to clean, silicone toys can be washed in very hot or boiling water, and you can even stick pure silicone dildos in the dishwasher (although this may not be a good idea if your dinner guests are helping you to stack it!). Handy tip: never use silicone- or oil-based lubricants with your silicone toy, as they can melt it.

PLASTIC
Another easy customer, simply rub with an antiseptic or alcohol wipe, or use a special sex-toy cleaner, available from sex shops. You can also use ordinary soap and water, but remove the batteries and wrap a towel around the base first, to avoid getting liquid inside.

METAL
This can be washed, boiled, or rubbed with soap or disinfectant. Easy!

JELLY, RUBBER, AND LATEX
While softer materials feel great against your skin, they're also very porous, so need to be cleaned carefully, to prevent bacteria from growing. Harsh or abrasive cleaners will harm the surface, so only use a special toy cleaner, or warm water and a very mild facial soap.

OVER TO YOU...

I asked five women to reveal all about their sex-toy-induced orgasms:

I'd never had the guts to try sex toys before I got together with my current boyfriend. He's surprisingly kinky, and after a couple of months of being together, he dragged me into a sex shop. We bought a selection of toys, and I have to say, it totally opened my eyes. My favorite is a fairly basic, silver plastic vibrator. It's not too scary-looking, and my boyfriend uses it on me before we have sex, so I'm always guaranteed to have an orgasm. I can't believe it's taken me so long to get into things like this.

    Louisa, 26

I bought a duck vibrator after seeing it in a magazine. I tried it underwater, but it didn't really work, as the water washed away my natural lubrication—but when I tried it "on land," the results were amazing. I rub the smooth head over my clitoris, and I climax within minutes.

    Hannah, 29

I was given a Rabbit vibrator by a friend. I thought it might be painful because of its size, but it wasn't at all—it's sensational! When I put all the settings on at once, I have the best orgasms ever.

    Sam, 24

My boyfriend and I recently tried out a vibrating cock ring. Not only did it buzz against my clitoris, making me come during sex—which hardly ever happens normally—but my boyfriend really loved it too, as he said it made his balls tin-

gle. Sadly, the battery ran out after just one session, but we plan to invest in another one very soon!

HELEN, 24

I've taken the whole sex-toy thing one step at a time. I started with a pink, finger-shaped vibrator, and have upgraded to my first Rabbit and a special minty lubricant. I don't like putting toys inside me, though—it's too uncomfortable—so instead, I hold them over my vagina, which gives me an incredibly intense climax.

JO, 28

Chapter 8
LET ME BE YOUR FANTASY

My best ever orgasm...
My fiancé, Richard, was always extolling the virtues of outdoor sex, but I wasn't keen, until one day when we had a picnic. After a few drinks, he hinted at having sex right there on the grass. We did, and although the park was quite quiet, the thrill we could get caught sent us wild. It opened my eyes, and now I'm more experimental!
Caroline, 22

FANTASIES—GOOD, CLEAN FUN

Unless you're a professional erotic fiction writer or mens' mag cover star, most of us are too frozen by fear to admit we even have fantasies, let alone tell someone else about them. Whenever you're playing a drunken game of "Spin the Bottle," or an enlightened man asks the dreaded, "So, what's your fantasy?" question in bed, we stutter and blush, before coming out with something completely unoriginal—and untrue—like, "Um, being blindfolded with a silk scarf while you ravish me?" before desperately trying to change the subject. It's a shame—especially given that studies have shown 95 percent of us have sexual fantasies daily... and yes, that means your mom probably does, too! But while she might be wondering what's beneath the plumber's oily overalls, you may well be imagining doing unspeakably rude things to Daniel Craig, the man next door, or the guy from finance. You see, fantasies don't have to be scary, sexually adventurous S&M-style ordeals (though that's not to rule those out); they're just a creative expression of our sensuality and can be triggered by sight, smell, touch, or sound—anything that stimulates your imagination.

It's a common myth that people who fantasize aren't satisfied with their real-life sex life, but the opposite is actually true. Experts reckon those who fantasize the most are likely to be those having the most sex—and great sex at that. Daydreaming during sex or while masturbating doesn't mean your real-life partner is boring or lacking in the bedroom department, and it doesn't mean you'd necessarily like your fantasies to come true. It's basically just a way of having no-strings-attached, guilt-free fun.

In fact, your fantasies are one of your orgasm's best friends. Firstly, they help to keep your mind focused on the job in hand. Picture the scene—you and your man are getting down to business, when you suddenly remember you've got a crisis meeting with your boss tomorrow, you need to get your new boots reheeled, and you haven't fed the cat. At moments like these, summoning up your favorite fantasy can get you back on track, pushing nonsexual thoughts to the back of your mind, and allowing you to enjoy what's happening to you right there and then.

Secondly, fantasies are great for getting you in the mood. Just thinking about sex can be a turn-on (that's why many experts say your mind is your biggest sexual organ), so whether you're indulging in a bit of solo sex, or getting frisky with your man, imagining a sexy scenario can get your juices flowing in double-quick time.

Fantasies are also a fantastic way of reaching climax when an orgasm is proving difficult. When it seems like you've been nearly-but-not-quite-there for ages, thinking of something filthy can add an extra spark of excitement just when you need it most... finally tipping you over the edge. Still skeptical? Try it—you may be more than pleasantly surprised.

WHAT DOES YOUR SECRET SEX FANTASY MEAN?

Now that we've cleared that up, what exactly do your fantasies mean? And should you act them out, or keep them just as they are—fantasies? Read on...

SECRET SEX FANTASY 1—ROLE PLAYING

WHAT IT MEANS:
Whether you've heard about people playing doctors and nurses, played it yourself, or even just imagined yourself as a different character during sex, then you're familiar with sexual role playing. But what does bringing role play into the bedroom actually mean? Judi James, relationship expert, life coach, and author of *Sex Signals: Send and Decode Them,* says: "Sexual role playing is about allowing different sides of ourselves—ones that are perhaps restricted in normal life— to come out. In terms of your sex life, this means you are ready and willing to push the parameters of your personality and explore new territory."

Individual fantasies can also tell you specific things about what you're looking for in your sex life, too.

IF YOU FANTASIZE ABOUT... BEING A PROSTITUTE

Don't panic, it doesn't mean you actually want to be a Belle de Jour type, so don't go out and buy those fishnets and see-through plastic shoes just yet! You're simply yearning for sex that's free of commitments, and restricts your emotional involvement. "Women are programmed to think sex has to involve emotion, otherwise we are publicly branded as prostitutes," Judi explains. "It's about tuning out that emotional attachment and focusing on the physical side of sex." Having this fantasy when in a relationship shows you're comfortable with exploring a sexual persona that's opposite to your own.

IF YOU FANTASIZE ABOUT...
BEING A LADY OF THE MANOR

Think *Desperate Housewives*. Lucky Gabrielle regularly had her wicked way with John the gardener, but many women can only dream of being ravished by a fit, nimble-fingered fella. And, boy, do we. This type of fantasy comes from the desire to be selfish and in control, and wanting a shift in the traditional power balance. Imagining yourself as the economically powerful one allows you to treat him as a slave, which in turn means he's at the mercy of your desire. Judi points out, "Having this fantasy means you'd like

the opportunity to be assertive in bed occasionally, but it doesn't mean you want that role all the time. It reflects a well-balanced sex life that has a good sense of fun present."

FANTASY TO REALITY?

Don't feel under pressure to dress up to act out a role play. It can be just as sexy (and less cringeworthy) if you only act out a conversation.

Do wait until things have started to heat up before you initiate a bit of role-play dialogue.

Don't turn it into any form of criticism. If you say, "I would like to be in charge, for once," he might think you're unhappy with what he's doing. Remember, men's egos are easily bruised. Suggest things as a question, not a statement.

Do make a point of saying if you don't want to act out the role play, but just enjoy talking about it.

SECRET SEX FANTASY 2—SEX WITH YOUR PARTNER

WHAT IT MEANS:

It's very common for people in long-term relationships to fantasize about sex with their own partner, because they have the confidence and trust to be experimental. Besides, the attainable is much more erotic than the unattainable, and fantasizing about doing things you've never tried is heightened by the prospect that they could come true! It doesn't mean you lack imagination; in fact, it gives you the chance to let it run wild. Instead of focusing on whom you're doing it with, your energy is put into what you're doing with him. It's a very positive sign if you want to have sex only with your partner, although you should also take heed. "Some women fantasize about their partner doing different things while they're actually having sex with him, which could mean they're not fulfilled by the sex they're having. It might be a sign that it's time to start introducing new things," explains Judi. "Try talking to him about your fantasies, and ask him to tell you his. Make sure you say it's him you're fantasizing about, so he doesn't feel insecure."

FANTASY TO REALITY?

Don't feel ashamed or embarrassed. Fantasies are an essential part of sexual repertoire.

Do tread carefully—the turn-on may be talking about your fantasy, not acting it out.

Don't immediately throw in weird and wonderful sexual curve balls. You may freak him out—and if he does the same, it may make you want to run a mile! No matter how long you've been together, start simply.

Do let yourself go.

SECRET SEX FANTASY 3—SEX WITH A WOMAN

WHAT IT MEANS:

Many women fantasize about sex with another woman, so before you start trying to spot other signs of lady-loving leanings, remember that the majority of the time, this has nothing to do with lesbian urges, and lots to do with the fact you're looking for novel ways of approaching sex. It might be your man isn't giving you the type of sex you desire, particularly if the two of you don't see eye to eye when it comes to your sexual styles. In this case, the woman you're conjuring up is an extension of yourself—she's showing you how you'd like to be made love to.

FANTASY TO REALITY?

Don't worry about your sexuality (unless you really believe it's more deeply rooted).

Do tell your partner; he'll find it a big turn-on.

Don't tell all your girlfriends! They might think you desire them.

Do use your fantasy to help you understand the kind of sex you want to be having—and try to translate that to your partner.

SECRET SEX FANTASY 4—SEX WITH MORE THAN ONE PERSON

WHAT IT MEANS:
It's always assumed that men fantasize more about three-somes than women, but while it is an obvious fantasy for men, that's not to say the thought of being ravished by the entire male cast of *Lost* isn't something any of us ladies haven't thought about, too. "These fantasies are all about sexual curiosity," Judi James explains. "They allow you to be desired by as many people as you like." Once again, it doesn't mean that you want others in your sex life, nor should you, necessarily—these things can end painfully when real people get involved. But it's a positive fantasy, all the same. You're imagining yourself as the focus of these people's attention, which makes you feel good about yourself. It also shows sexual confidence, as it's about giving two or more people your body.

IF YOU FANTASIZE ABOUT... SEX WITH TWO MEN
This fantasy is all about you being totally pleasured. But your boyfriend needn't worry. "This isn't so much a sign that your partner isn't satisfying you," Judi explains, "but more a sign that you'd like two of your own partner. It shows you're very into the physical side of sex and want every part of your body to be pleasured simultaneously."

IF YOU FANTASIZE ABOUT... SEX WITH YOUR PARTNER AND ANOTHER WOMAN

"This isn't actually an indication you have bisexual tendencies, but a sign you're keen to give your boyfriend the biggest turn-on possible," says Judi. A lot of the time when women fantasize about being with another woman, their partner is watching. "The big finale usually involves the man joining in and it becomes more about him," she adds.

IF YOU FANTASIZE ABOUT... BEING WATCHED OR WATCHING OTHERS HAVING SEX

You only have to look at the viewing figures of *Big Brother* to know we're all voyeurs. The thrill of fantasies like these is knowing there's someone watching you—it shows your bedroom antics are worth viewing!

IF YOU FANTASIZE ABOUT... SWINGING

According to Judi James, having a fantasy about partner-swapping can be a sign of a recent sexual epiphany; you may have become more sexually aware.

FANTASY TO REALITY?

Don't convince yourself you need to carry out the fantasy. Most people get their kicks from just talking about it, knowing it won't go any further than that.

Do turn off the light and use a fantasy dialogue. Imagine yourselves in the scenario, and then say things like, "Tell me what you'd be doing to X now..."

Don't indulge in the fantasy until you're sure you both understand it's just that.

SECRET SEX FANTASY 5—DOMINATION/SUBMISSION

WHAT IT MEANS:

Most fantasies take the form of one person being dominant (in control) and the other submissive (obedient)—especially during role plays. Many people confuse these fantasies with sleazy S&M-type images, which gives them a seedy edge, but, according to Judi James, if you often fantasize about being dominant in bed, it shows you're in a relationship that is comfortable. "Many of these fantasies involve a great deal of trust," explains Judi. "But they can also show a desire to take control of your sex life and have the chance to show him exactly what you like."

Having a fantasy where you are utterly submissive is about intense sexual trust. "It's like saying to your partner, 'You can do anything you like to me and I know I'll like it,'" says Judi. In fact, you could go so far as to say that domination/submission fantasies, like being tied up by your partner, are actually a metaphor for wanting to be tied to your partner long-term.

FANTASY TO REALITY?

Don't go out and buy bondage gear, thinking that's the only way to act out this type of fantasy. There are gentler ways that won't involve you setting foot in a hard-core sex shop. Do swap roles, so you can try it both ways.

Don't tell the world what you're doing. Treat it as a naughty secret.

Do think of stock phrases, so if you feel tongue-tied when you're, ahem, tied up, you can use them without embarrassment.

Do have a safe "stop" word, so if one of you becomes un-comfortable with what's going on, you both know it's time to halt proceedings.

OVER TO YOU...

I asked five extremely frank women to reveal their deepest, darkest fantasies...

I'm married to someone the same age as me, but I fantasize about having sex with a much older man—perhaps in his late forties—who's really taken care of his body over the years, and has sexy silver hair. I imagine he'd be incredibly experi-enced, confident, and uninhibited, and he'd show me the time of my life in bed. I'm making sure my husband stays in shape, so perhaps in twenty years' time, my fantasy will come true!

JEMMA, 28

I dream about having sex in a field of long grass on a spring evening in the rain with a very sexy woman. I've never really tried to make it come true, although I did kiss a woman once, and imagined my fantasy while I did so.

MICHELLE ANNE, 26

My ultimate fantasy would be getting tied up during sex. I'd wake up in the middle of the night to find my wrists and ankles bound with silk ties to the bedposts—and a sexy stranger rubbing me all over with baby oil. I've never felt comfortable enough with my past boyfriends to try it out, though—but I live in hope...

CAROLINE, 25

My number-one turn-on has always been the idea of being with someone I shouldn't. Whether it's someone in authority, like my boss; a professor; a married man; or a friend's brother, father, or even boyfriend! Of course, none of these would be a great idea to carry out in real life, so I don't tend to fulfill them.

DEBBIE, 22

My favorite fantasy is to make love on the beach at sunset, and not stop until sunrise. I've done this several times now— it's amazing how quickly you learn to dodge the sand! I've had several other fantasies over the years, like having sex in public, in a swimming pool, threesomes, etc., and as I'm very sexually open, I talked to my partners about it, and we've fulfilled nearly everything on my list.

ELEANOR, 30

Chapter 9
THE ORGASM WORKOUT

MY BEST EVER ORGASM...
I've been doing Pilates, and one of the things we learned was pelvic floor exercises. You clench and unclench your vaginal muscles, practicing through peeing and stopping midstream. It's done wonders for my sex life, as I can now contract my muscles for ultra-powerful orgasms.
   CHLOE, 27

A SMALL AMOUNT OF EFFORT CAN MAKE A BIG DIFFERENCE

When you want your legs looking extra hot in a mini-skirt, you hit the Thighmaster. When you want to run a marathon, you start going on training runs. And when you want blow-your-socks-off orgasms? Yes, you guessed it: you've got to exercise.

Unfortunately, as with everything in life, truly great orgasms require a bit of effort. But, luckily, you don't need to make the gym your second home to get results. It's not about changing your body shape, or working out until your abs are so taut you could bounce peanuts off them—instead, it's about retraining your muscles, opening up your body, and unlearning bad habits. All you need are a few moves here, a change in breathing technique there, and you'll be hitting the big O without even breaking a sweat (well, almost).

Interested? Practice the moves and techniques in this chapter for a few weeks, and I promise you'll never think of exercise as being boring again...

SOMETHING INSIDE SO STRONG

Forget your inner thighs—when it comes to orgasms, many sexperts would argue the most important muscles in your body are your pelvic floor muscles. Officially known as the pubococcygeus or PC muscles, they form a kind of sling inside you, and support your vagina, urethra, and rectum. They're the parts you can feel contracting and releasing during climax. Want to locate them? The next time you go to the toilet, stop peeing midstream. The muscles you use to do this are your pelvic floor muscles.

Exercises for these mini-miracles (often called kegel exercises, after Dr. Arnold Kegel, a famous gynecologist) are usually recommended to women who've just given birth, and need to tighten things up down below. But they've got another, saucier use, too. Strengthening your pelvic floor can literally transform your sex life—not only should your orgasms feel stronger and your vagina more sensitive, but you'll have more control when your man is inside you, and flexing them may even help you get aroused more quickly—which can only be a good thing.

The really great news is kegels are easy to do, and you can practice them anywhere—in your car, at your desk, or at the local wine bar—and no one will be any the wiser.

How do I do them? Sitting or lying down, squeeze and release your pelvic floor muscles twenty times, while breathing normally. It's as simple as that!

How do I know I'm doing them right? Put your hand on your stomach—your stomach muscles shouldn't move, and neither should your legs, back, or bottom muscles. Strangely, sucking on a pen, teaspoon, or your thumb can help, but don't worry if you find it difficult at first—you'll get better with practice.

How often should I practice? Start with just one set of twenty contractions a day, then buildup to forty; and begin holding each squeeze for a couple of seconds before releasing. Do your kegels every day and you should notice a difference after just three weeks.

Do I need any exercise equipment? No, although some women who want to take things further use special toys, gadgets, cones, and dildos to help with their kegels. They're available from online female-friendly sex shops. Alternatively, ask your doctor to refer you to a gynecologist.

How can I make them harder? Try holding the contraction for five to ten seconds before releasing; or do them standing up—you'll have to work harder, as you're fighting against gravity.

Can I practice with my man? Oh, yes. Try squeezing and releasing your muscles down below when your man is inside you, during sex. Not only will this help you locate the right muscles, but it'll also make his penis feel amazing. He'll be more than happy to help you out on a regular basis!

SIX ORGASMIC SEX-ERCISES

1. FOR HAPPY HIPS

Your hips and pelvis see a lot of action in the bedroom, but they're often neglected during normal exercise. So, show them a bit of TLC—your orgasms will thank you for it!

The ultimate exercise: Stand up straight, with your feet shoulder-width apart, your knees slightly bent and your hands resting lightly on your hips. Slowly rotate your hips clockwise, like a belly dancer, as if they were making a circle. Inhale and squeeze your pelvic floor muscles (see kegel exercises, page 123) as you swivel your body forward; then exhale and relax your muscles as you move it back. After ten full rotations, stop, and then do ten more in an anticlockwise direction. Practice daily, building up to twenty rotations in each direction.

Why it's worth it: The looser your hips, the more you'll be able to rotate them and grind against your man during sex, so your clitoris gets maximum attention. You'll also find it easier to get into any sexual position you want.

Want more? Try belly-dancing classes for a sexy wiggle, improved body confidence, and rock-hard abs.

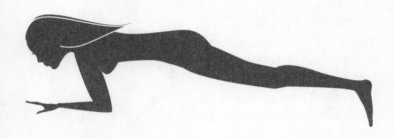

2. FOR INNER STRENGTH

Your core muscles form a band deep inside your body, reaching from the bottom of your ribs to your pelvis, and your abs around to your spine—a bit like an internal corset. They're vital for every move you make, and help keep you stable and balanced, particularly during sex.

The ultimate exercise: To give them a workout, start by lying face down on a mat, towel, or rug, with your arms bent at the elbows, and your hands by your shoulders, palms downward. Next, lift your body off the floor, as if you were going to do a push-up. Your entire body weight should now be resting on just your toes and hands (or forearms, if you find it easier). Suck in your stomach, and keep your body in a straight line from your head to your toes. Hold this position for ten seconds. Practice daily, building up to holding for a maximum of thirty seconds at a time.

Why it's worth it: Strong core muscles not only help you support yourself when you're on top or having sex standing up, but they'll make your orgasmic contractions stronger, too.

Want more? Balance-ball exercises are excellent for core muscles—even just sitting on one forces you to use them correctly. Alternatively, ask your personal trainer to demonstrate the best moves for you.

3. FOR FLEXIBILITY

Great sex is all about fluid, easy movements—not so great for those of us with desk jobs, whose bodies are creakier than warped floorboards. To test your flexibility, stand up straight, then bend at the waist and try to touch your toes without bending your knees. If you find this even slightly difficult, you've got work to do.

The ultimate exercise: Get down on your hands and knees—as if you were crawling. Make sure your hands are shoulder-width apart and your legs are hip-width apart. Then tilt your bottom upwards, so your spine curves downward. At the same time, inhale and look up at the ceiling. Hold for a couple of seconds, then exhale and look down, tilting your pelvis downward, and your spine up. Keep your stomach tucked in as you do so. Do three repetitions, several times a week.

Why it's worth it: The more flexible you are, the deeper the angle of penetration, and the more likely it is your man will hit your hot spots. You'll also be able to get into, and hold, trickier sexual positions with ease.

Want more? Take up yoga. It increases the flexibility of every limb in your body—oh, and the breathing techniques will help to improve your orgasms, too.

4. FOR LEGS OF STEEL

You use your legs more than you'd imagine during sex. Toning them will not only improve your sex life, though—you'll look better in shorts, too!

The ultimate exercise: Get down on your hands and knees—as if you were crawling. Make sure your hands are shoulder-width apart and your legs are hip-width apart. With your back straight and your stomach pulled in, lower yourself down on to your elbows. Next, keeping your knee bent, and squeezing your bottom muscles as you do so, lift your right foot upwards towards the ceiling, until your thigh is parallel to the floor. Slowly lower your leg to the starting position. After ten repetitions, repeat with your left leg. Practice daily, building up to three sets of ten on each side. A favorite with aerobics instructors, this exercise will also work your bottom!

Why it's worth it: Strong legs are a real bonus in many sexual positions, and some sexperts believe your hamstrings are linked to your pelvic floor muscles—so giving them a workout could prove surprisingly beneficial.

Want more? Get on your bike, or join a gym's spinning class. As well as working your legs, you'll improve your cardiovascular fitness—vital for bedroom stamina.

5. FOR UPPER BODY STRENGTH

Your triceps are the muscles at the backs of your arms—or to give them their unofficial name, bingo wings. Toning them up has more life-changing benefits than simply helping you to look good in tank tops...

The ultimate exercise:
Tricep dips are incredibly easy to do and get quick results. Start by sitting on the edge of a chair, step, bed, or even the bath, with your arms straight by your sides and your hands curled around the edge. Stretch your legs out in front of you, with your knees slightly bent and your feet flat on the floor. Slowly lift your bottom forward off the edge of the chair, keeping your arms straight, until they're taking all your weight. This is the

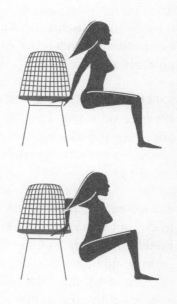

starting position. Next, lower your body by slowly bending your elbows—make sure they point in a straight line behind you, rather than moving out to the sides. Keep your bottom close to the edge of the chair as you dip, and stop several inches off the ground—before your arms reach a 90-degree angle, or you feel any strain in your shoulders. Then slowly straighten your arms and return to the starting position. Don't forget to breathe—exhale on the way down, and inhale on the way up. Do fifteen to twenty repetitions, a couple of times a week.

Why it's worth it: Strong arms make standing-up sex, woman-on-top positions, and rocking movements easy. Which means you can hang on for the orgasm you deserve, without getting shaky muscles halfway through.

Want more? Free weights are one of the quickest ways to buildup the muscles in your arms. Ask your gym instructor to show you his muscles, (sorry), and how to use them properly and effectively.

6. FOR THIGHS, HIPS, AND BOTTOM

It's time we stopped seeing our bottom halves as problem areas. The muscles here are surprisingly strong and it takes only a few minutes' exercise each day to get them working in your favor.

The ultimate exercise: Squats are easy to do, but don't let that fool you—there's no better way to tone your bottom and thighs. Start by standing in front of a chair, with your hands resting lightly on your hips, your feet hip-width apart, and your knees soft and flexible. Keeping your back straight throughout, slowly bend your knees and squat down, as if you were going to sit on the chair. Just as your bottom grazes the top of it, stop.

Now stand back up again by straightening your legs, squeezing your bottom as you return to the starting position. Repeat twelve times. Buildup to three sets, two or three times a week. A couple of safety points: never curve or bend your back, and always keep your knees in line with your toes, rather than letting them bend further forward. Want to make it harder? Try holding a pole weight over your shoulders, milkmaid-style; a barbell clutched to your chest; or grip two hand-held weights by your sides.

Why it's worth it: Not only do strong buttocks and thighs help when you want to squat over your man during sex, but if you squeeze them together just as you're reaching climax, you may find the action helps to tip you over the edge into orgasm more quickly.

Want more? Kickboxing or boxercise classes are a great way to get a toned lower half. Focus on high-kicking moves for maximum benefits.

AND BREATHE...

The tension's building, you can feel your excitement peaking, you're almost there... so you hold your breath to help squeeze out that orgasm, right? Wrong. It's only natural to want to hold your breath as you tense your muscles ready for the big O, but doing this will actually make orgasm less likely. What your body needs right now is oxygen—and lots of it.

Oxygen is vital for every cell in our bodies to function. During sex, all the muscles in your body get a workout—

particularly those in your legs, pelvic region, and genitals. In order to work efficiently, they need fuel in the form of oxygen. But oxygen doesn't just help your stamina during sex—it also increases your circulation, speeds up your metabolism, helps your body stay relaxed (essential for orgasm), and keeps your brain focused on what's happening in your nether regions.

The problem is, most of us are lazy breathers. Anyone who's ever heard a screaming baby can attest to the fact that we're born knowing how to breathe and use our lungs properly; but as we grow older, we forget this, and begin to use only the top part of our lungs, taking shallow breaths instead of normal, deeper ones. Relearning how to breathe deeply—and doing so at the point of orgasm—can increase the amount of oxygen your body gets, and therefore improve your sex life, tenfold. And the good news is, it's easy to do.

First, identify your breathing style. Sit or stand up straight, or lie flat on your back on the floor. Place one hand on your stomach and breathe as you would normally, noticing whether your chest, or your hand, rises up. If your chest rises, you've got room for improvement.

PRACTICE THE FOLLOWING EXERCISE ONCE A DAY:

Step 1: Slowly breathe in through your nose for a count of five, trying to push your hand upwards with your stomach as it fills with air.

Step 2: Now hold your breath for a count of five.

Step 3: Next, breathe out through your mouth for a count of five, while slowly pushing down on your stomach with your hand.

Step 4: Repeat steps 1 to 3 for one minute.

Increase the length of time you practice for, until you can manage at least five minutes at a stretch. Do this regularly, and before long, you'll find you're breathing properly through your stomach like this, without thinking, all day long.

Chapter 10
FAKING IT

My best ever orgasm...
I used to get really uptight when I was unable to orgasm during sex. After one too many mediocre sessions, I confided in my friend, Becki. She used to have exactly the same problem, but once she'd learned to focus on the joys of foreplay and experimented with various positions—instead of worrying about the climax—she had much more fun. She made me realize that great sex isn't just about the big O. Mind you, ever since I took Becki's advice, I've had many more orgasms, anyway!
Leigh, 26

WHY ARE YOU FAKING IT?

Which three-word phrase, apart from, "Where's the door?" is the worst thing a man can utter straight after sex? It is, of course, "Did you come?" If you didn't and you say yes, you're lying, and likely to feel guilty. But saying no can be just as bad—not only do you feel a failure, but your man feels pretty inadequate, too.

Why do we feel like this? Why, instead of simply accepting—and admitting—that sometimes we're just not going to come, do we pretend to climax, or end up muttering excuses like, "It's not you, it must be me," or, "I'm sorry, I'm just really tired tonight," as though we've committed some kind of sexual sin?

There are any number of reasons—just check out the top-ten sex spoilers on the next few pages, for starters—but one of the biggest by far is because we think we ought to orgasm every time. Orgasm has become something to aim for in every sexual encounter—we get fixated on it, telling ourselves that sex is a letdown without one. It's a shame, because in focusing on the end result, we miss out on all the fun we could be having along the way. And the irony is, the more you will yourself to reach orgasm, the less likely it is to happen.

Men are just as guilty of this tunnel vision, if not more so. They believe if they don't make their partner come, their bedroom skills are somehow lacking. We women are aware of this approach, so we fake orgasm to avoid hurting our man's feelings. Or we fake it because we know he'll keep banging away until he gets the response he's looking for, which can, after sixty minutes of staring at the ceiling, get boring.

So here they are, the hard facts. Men are practically guaranteed an orgasm every time they have sex, but women are different. It takes us a lot longer, and the conditions have to be just right, for us to reach the big O. Add to this the fact that sex therapists say on average, out of every ten sexual encounters with the same partner, you'll find two are fantastic, two are awful, and six will be just a little better or worse than average, and it makes perfect sense why women don't orgasm every time. Accepting this—and getting your man to accept it too—is the key to stopping faking forever.

LITTLE WHITE LIE, OR GREAT BIG WHOPPER?

If you're a serial faker, you're not alone. In a survey of *Company* magazine readers, a staggering 70 percent of women claimed to have faked an orgasm at least once in their lives: 17 percent of these said it was a one-off; 39 percent had done it a handful of times; 28 percent used to fake regularly with their ex, but no longer do so with their new partner; and 5 percent admitted they faked orgasm every single time they had sex.

If we're all faking it occasionally, it begs the question: is the odd pretend orgasm *really* that bad? Sexperts are split on the issue. Some say faking is like telling a little white lie. If 95 percent of your orgasms are bona fide, the odd fake one (when you're tired, say) is perfectly acceptable, as you're only doing it to save your partner's feelings. Others, however, say any pretense in bed is damaging to your relationship, as it's breaking the bond of trust, and could be the start of a vicious circle. If you appear to come every time you have sex, your man will begin to expect it, and you'll feel under yet more pressure to keep coming up with the goods (as it were). And, should you stay together long-term, if your man ever finds out you've been pretending for years, you'll hurt his feelings way more than if you'd just admitted to not coming occasionally in the first place.

RETRAINING YOUR MAN

If you're entering into a new relationship, you can avoid the faking trap by being honest from the start. Explain you don't always orgasm during sex, but that's okay, because you don't have to—it's simply an added (albeit extremely nice) bonus. Begin as you mean to go on and, hopefully, you'll begin to relax fully in bed—you may even find you have more orgasms than you did before.

If you've been together for a while, though, suddenly telling your man you don't always orgasm during sex can be a little tricky. So, broach the subject tactfully. Start by being more open with him generally, telling him after sex what you loved, and what you would have liked more of. Then, once he's used to the idea of you talking about sex, suggest some new positions to try in bed together (chapter six has plenty of examples). If you don't come in these positions, say so. Explain that while you were extremely turned on, and you'd like to try it again, you didn't climax—does your man have any suggestions for how it could be better next time? Talk through the possible reasons why your orgasm eluded you: maybe he said something that made you lose concentration just before you peaked; maybe you felt you needed more lubrication; or maybe you weren't relaxed enough. He won't be surprised, or hurt, because it's something neither of you have tried before.

You can then move on from here, experimenting with different techniques, until you find something that works. He'll also get used to the idea that you can enjoy sex without the big finale; and once the pressure's off, you can start having the sex life you deserve.

TOP-TEN SEX SPOILERS

Sex on the silver screen is smooth and seamless. Everyone looks beautiful, the lighting is soft, the sheets are pure Egyptian cotton, and couples want to rip each other's clothes off 24/7. Real sex isn't like this—everyday stuff tends to get in the way, meaning you're sometimes more likely to win the lottery than climax. When this happens, it's tempting just to summon up your best acting skills and fake it. But what if there was an easy way to fix these common sex spoilers, and guarantee real orgasms every time? Here's how to make sure the top-ten orgasm enemies never get in the way of your climax again...

YOU FAKE IT BECAUSE... YOU WANT IT TOO MUCH

Orgasms are elusive little fellas—in order to have one, your body and mind need to be completely relaxed and "in tune." It stands to reason that the more you think about having an orgasm, the less likely it is to happen—you tense up, you get distracted, and all the pleasurable feelings you've been having get lost in a haze of frustration and disappointment. So, you end up faking it.

How to get real: You need to change the way you think about orgasms. Stop seeing them as something you have to achieve in order to have great sex, and start seeing them as lottery scratchcards—it's fantastic if you win, but if you don't, you can still have fun playing! Concentrate on the fun side of sex, the intimacy it creates between you and your man, and the spine-tingling sensations you experience; your orgasms will come when they're ready.

YOU FAKE IT BECAUSE... YOU'RE SELF-CONSCIOUS

We've all been there. You're just getting into your stride when you realize, with horror, that your thighs are wobbling like jelly, your stomach's dangling dangerously over your man's head, and your boobs are swinging around like two half-deflated balloons. There's no surer passion-killer than feeling insecure about your body in bed... so you quickly clench your body and moan loudly, just to divert his attention away from your wobbly parts, and on to his penis. Phew—that was close.

How to get real: Firstly, remind yourself that your man wouldn't be in bed with you if he didn't find you sexy. Secondly, rather than drawing your man's attention to your less-than-perfect body, get the ball rolling by telling him all the things you like about his body; and then ask him to tell you what he likes about yours. The answers may be pleasantly surprising!

YOU FAKE IT BECAUSE... YOU'RE STRESSED

Orgasms start in your brain, so if your man gets frisky when you've had a hard day at work, or you're worrying about the state of your bank balance, your mind won't be on the job in hand. It's practically impossible to have an orgasm if you're thinking about something entirely nonsexual—by the time you snap back to reality and realize your poor boyfriend has been plugging away for nearly an hour with no result, you'll both be wishing for a fake climax to bring the whole sorry situation to an end.

How to get real: Believe it or not, sex is one of the best cures for stress, as it releases mood-boosting hormones that make you feel positive and ready to tackle anything. Ask your man to give you a calming massage, take a bath together, or get him to read you a sexy story: these activities will bring your blood pressure down, relax your body, and ease your brain into sex, rather than stress, mode.

YOU FAKE IT BECAUSE... YOU'RE TOO DRY

Women need, on average, at least twenty minutes of foreplay before they're sufficiently aroused to achieve orgasm. During this time, your body produces natural secretions to help his penis slip comfortably inside you. If your man enters you before you're ready, it's likely you'll feel sore—and the big O will be the last thing on your mind. Other causes of vaginal dryness include some types of contraceptive Pill, hormone changes at certain points in your menstrual cycle, and perfumed soaps and shower gels. This is a really common cause of bedroom dissatisfaction and many women pretend they've come just to make the friction stop.

How to get real: There's an easy way around this one. Either insist on more foreplay (getting him to go down on you should definitely help move things along a little) or, if you're desperate for a quickie, help yourself to a dollop or two of man-made, water-based lubricant, like K-Y Jelly. Done!

YOU FAKE IT BECAUSE... HIS TECHNIQUE IS OFF

Sadly, not all men are born sex gods. Hands up if you recognize this situation: you're in bed and your man is tweaking your nipples like radio dials; pumping away like he's inflating a car tire; or massaging your vagina so hard it's like he's sanding wood. It's all about as erotic and exciting as descaling a showerhead. Hopefully, this happens only with a new man, but even long-term partners are guilty of, ahem, rubbing you up the wrong way. How do you make it stop? You fake it, of course. And quite frankly, who can blame you?

How to get real: Your man needs guidance. But rather than barking instructions at him like a traffic cop, gently move his hand to where you want it, or utter something like, "I love it when you touch me there, like that," to encourage good behavior. Alternatively, if you're feeling brave, take matters into your own hands and show him exactly how you like to be touched, by giving him a ringside seat the next time you indulge in a little solo sex.

YOU FAKE IT BECAUSE... YOU'RE JUST NOT IN THE MOOD

Sometimes, your hormones are to blame. Sometimes, it's because you've got an early start the next morning and want your beauty sleep. Or the *Sex and the City* marathon is about to start. Whatever the reason, occasionally you're just not up for sex, period. Men, however, as the saying goes, think about sex every six seconds (yes, even in the middle of *Law & Order*). So what do you do if your other half gets frisky in these situations? Rather than push him off and cause a fight, you agree to get down to business, but pretend you've climaxed in double-quick time. He's happy, and you can watch the second half of your favorite program in peace, right? Wrong.

How to get real: You've got a couple of options. If you think you might be up for sex later, say so, and suggest the two of you just cuddle for now. Or, you could tell him how sexy you find watching him pleasure himself— and get him to give you a little floor show. That way, he's satisfied, and you don't have to demonstrate your acting prowess. Alternatively, you could just tell him you think he's gorgeous, and you love getting down and dirty with him, but right now, you wouldn't be great company in the sack. If he looks miffed, offer him a cuddle or massage as a consolation prize, and make sure you initiate things the next time.

YOU FAKE IT BECAUSE... THE ATMOSPHERE'S WRONG

It's hard to feel sexy when your roommate's got her stereo on full blast in the room next door; your man's bedroom looks like a bomb's hit it; or the lighting is so severe you feel like you're in a department-store changing room. Some women can have sex anywhere, in any situation—but most of us need a bit of peace and quiet, and the right setting, to really let go and enjoy ourselves. However, rather than admitting your man's overflowing laundry basket is dampening your ardor, it's more tempting to take the less embarrassing option and fake it—then leave him lying there while you leap out of bed to switch on the washing machine.

How to get real: Preparation's what you need. Change your 100-watt light-bulbs to softer, 40-watt ones; try to initiate sex when your roommate's out for the night; and suggest your man gives his room a spring clean (tell him if it felt like a boudoir, you'd want sex even more often—then sit back and watch him make best friends with the Hoover!). Once you can truly relax, your orgasms should come naturally.

YOU FAKE IT BECAUSE... YOU'RE TIRED

Tiredness is another huge orgasm-killer. Your body just doesn't function properly when you're exhausted—after all, if you can hardly stay awake, how can you have an orgasm? But saying, "Not tonight, darling, I'm tired," sounds like such a cliché, it seems easier to agree to sex and fake it. That way, you can both roll over and go to sleep afterwards, no questions asked.

How to get real: If you really don't want to hurt your man's feelings by turning him down gently—and if he's a reasonable guy, he honestly won't mind—then try sleepy sex. Tell your man you're less than bright-eyed and bushy-tailed, and suggest a minimum-effort position, like Spoons (see page 83), where he lies behind you and does all the work. With any luck, you should both get an orgasm, and as you're already in bed, you don't even have to move afterwards.

YOU FAKE IT BECAUSE... IT HURTS

Sex + pain = no orgasms. But rather than admit there's something wrong down below, many women who find sex hurts choose to fake an orgasm instead. This does no one any favors at all. You're still in pain, and to make matters worse, you now feel guilty for lying.

How to get real: Sex can hurt for all kinds of physical, medical, and psychological reasons—read the next chapter for a detailed list. But there's no need to suffer in silence: make an appointment with your family-planning clinic, doctor, or local health clinic. The answer could be as simple as taking a course of antibiotics. And don't feel embarrassed—they've seen and heard it all before.

YOU FAKE IT BECAUSE... YOU'RE WORRIED ABOUT GETTING PREGNANT

A surprisingly common passion-killer, the fear of getting pregnant has caused many a woman to fake her climax. Orgasms require a clear head, so if you're panicking mid-thrust because you've, um, forgotten to use a condom, you're using one, but you're worried it's not on properly, or you suddenly remember you've not taken your Pill this morning, you're never going to reach the big O.

How to get real: Men are good at many things (fixing cars, killing spiders...), but organizing contraception isn't one of them. That's not to say they should be let off the hook—but the only real way to be confident you're protected against pregnancy is to sort out the matter yourself. If you have problems remembering to take the Pill, try the contraceptive injection or implant, both of which last for months at a time. If your man always forgets to bring condoms, slip a couple in your handbag. If he refuses to use contraception at all, it might be time to start looking for his replacement...

OVER TO YOU...

I asked five women to 'fess up to their bedroom dramatics—and tell me what they've discovered is the key to having real, bona fide orgasms every time.

I WAS INEXPERIENCED

I used to fake my orgasms, because I was inexperienced and didn't really know what to do in bed.

MY KEY TO HAVING REAL ORGASMS IS...
For me, it's having sex with the right partner. I've only ever experienced orgasm with my husband—it's because I'm uninhibited and very comfortable having sex with him, so I don't feel self-conscious, as I did with previous partners.

TINA, 26

I HAD A LOW SEX DRIVE
I fake it all the time! I've only ever had two sexual relationships. The first one started when I was nineteen and lasted four years—I faked it during this time because I'd lost interest in him and wanted to get it over with quickly. I had a low sex drive due to depression, and had difficulty achieving orgasm even by myself towards the end of the relationship, so it was easier to lie than spend forever seeking the unobtainable.

My current relationship, with a young guy who's only eighteen, has been going for a year—I fake it with him only because it stops him trying so hard. Once he thinks I've come, we can just relax and enjoy sex, and then I do get a real orgasm. I love having sex with him, and it's in no way a bad reflection on him that I fake it. I'm just a bit of a drama queen, and it makes him feel good thinking I'm coming over and over again. It also makes me feel good, because I enjoy the game leading up to my usually incredible, real orgasm."

MY KEY TO REAL ORGASMS IS...
Actually being mentally and physically turned on—wanting and allowing it to happen. The best positions for me are not ones that involve thrusting, but rather grinding movements, so there's complete contact between your genitals—and your clit rubs on the base of his penis as he moves inside you. The closeness of it is even more of a turn-on, plus you can feel his balls pulsing as he comes inside you.

KATY, 24

I DIDN'T WANT TO HURT HIM
I've faked orgasms—mainly because I didn't want to hurt my partner's feelings.

MY KEY TO REAL ORGASMS IS...
I've found the way to have an orgasm nearly every time is to thrust at the same time as my partner—that way, he enters me deeper, and sometimes my clitoris gets stimulated, too. It's very sexy, it turns me on that when he's about to orgasm, he gets very hard, and that makes me come too.
    ANN, 26

I WANTED TO GET IT OVER WITH
I admit I've faked orgasms. It sounds terrible, but the reason was I wanted to get the sex over with. I knew there was no chance of me having an orgasm, and I knew he wouldn't finish until he thought I'd had one!

MY KEY TO REAL ORGASMS IS...
I've learned that just relaxing and not worrying or stressing about orgasms makes you far more likely to have one.
    CAROL, 25

I GOT BORED
I've faked it only a few times—on the rare occasions that I just lost interest in what was going on, or he wouldn't orgasm till I did, and I was bored or wanted it to be over with. The funny thing is, despite men wanting us to think they don't care if we come or not, they do! Sometimes, you just have to pad their ego a bit.

MY KEY TO REAL ORGASMS IS...
Masturbation. You have to do it! Not only because, well, you can, so why wouldn't you?—but also because it gives you the

opportunity to find out what it is that you really like and need. Also, if you're not comfortable with yourself naked, or during sex, it gives you a chance to become more comfortable with your body in every way—to love it, to use it to your advantage, and to see what it can do. I think masturbation's one of the most important and effective ways of boosting your self-esteem.

DONNA, 29

Chapter 11
WHEN SEX HURTS

My best ever orgasm...
This is going to sound a bit medical, but the best orgasm I ever had was after an operation to ease my endometriosis. I'd been in a lot of pain for a long time, and to be honest, sex had become a bit of a chore. Having surgery was my last option and I was worried it might not work, but after waiting a couple of weeks to heal, the first time I had sex with my boyfriend afterwards, I couldn't believe the difference. As soon as I realized the pain had gone, I threw myself into sex, and it's just got better and better ever since.
BECKY, 28

SOMETIMES, SEX CAN BE A PAIN

When sex is more "ow" than "wow," there could be a simple reason—and an easy solution. Yet so many women put up with pain down below for weeks or even years before seeking advice. Alternatively, their doctors don't take them seriously. So, here's the lowdown on every passion-killer, from allergies to vaginismus—and a host of other conditions you probably didn't even know existed. If you find sex hurts, read up on the possible causes and take action—your body, your sex life, and your orgasms will thank you for it!

WHEN IT'S PHYSICAL...

YOUR BODY ISN'T READY YET

Within ten to thirty seconds of you getting frisky, two small glands on either side of your vagina begin secreting lubricating fluid to prepare you for penetration. The amount you produce, and how quickly you produce it, varies hugely from woman to woman. If your man enters you before you're properly aroused, it is, not surprisingly, going to feel pretty uncomfortable. Ask him to spend longer on foreplay before going for the "main event," or if you can't resist a quickie, use a dollop of lubricant to help things go more smoothly.

YOU'RE TOO CLEAN

Believe it or not, you can be too hygienic. Using vaginal cleansers or deodorants can upset your vagina's natural balance of healthy bacteria and reduce your natural lubrication. A healthy vagina should be self-cleansing, so all you really need to do is wash with water and an unscented soap or shower gel.

IT'S THE TIME OF THE MONTH

Just before and after ovulation, when your hormone levels rise, you'll produce less fluid when you get aroused, which can lead to friction during sex. During ovulation itself, some women's ovaries become super-sensitive. Your man might brush against them during sex, causing a sharp, stabbing pain deep inside. If you think this is the case, try switching positions to one that's more comfortable.

HE'S TOO BIG

Bigger isn't always better when it comes to his equipment. Your vagina should be able to accommodate any size of penis, but it can take a while to do so. As you get more aroused, your vagina lengthens and barrels out, and your cervix and womb tilt backwards and upwards. This can all take up to twenty-five minutes, so if your man is very well endowed and enters you too quickly, it can hurt. Plenty of foreplay and some artificial lubrication should help. The good news is, as you get more aroused, you'll continue to expand inside, so after the first few thrusts, even those men calling themselves Trousersnake should slip right in!

YOU'VE GOT AN ALLERGY

Spermicidal creams, perfumed toiletries, and the latex used to make condoms can all cause itching and swelling if you're allergic. Stick to unperfumed soaps and shower gels. If this sounds familiar and you think condoms are to blame, try switching to a brand without spermicide, or a polyurethane variety instead.

YOU'RE ON THE PILL

Some women find the Pill can cause vaginal dryness. Some brands lower your progesterone levels; progesterone is what keeps you moist down below. If you've recently started taking the Pill, or have switched brands, it'll take your body a few months to adjust, but if things don't improve, talk to your doctor about trying another. There are over twenty brands available, so there should be one to suit you.

IT'S JUST THE WAY YOU'RE MADE

While we all have the same equipment, it's not always arranged in exactly the same way. Some women find certain positions bring the cervix nearer to the vagina's entrance, making it more likely to get bashed by the tip of his penis during sex. Twenty percent of women also have a womb that tilts back slightly; some experts believe this may make sex more painful, as the ovaries can get caught between the vagina and the back of the pelvis, particularly in the missionary position. Try positions that don't involve lying on your back, although if your sex life is really suffering, an operation can solve the problem.

WHEN IT'S PSYCHOLOGICAL...

YOU'RE NOT RELAXED

Stress affects your estrogen levels—the hormone that controls your body's ability to get turned on. If you're not relaxed, you won't get properly aroused, and sex can be dry and painful. Any stress can be to blame—work, that fight you had with your mom, even sex itself (well, if you're worrying about him running a mile when he sees your wobbly body, you'll never relax!). Try concentrating on foreplay, or having a relaxing massage first, to get you in the mood.

YOU HAVE VAGINISMUS

Some women have deep, subconscious sexual worries, such as relationship problems, a fear of pain during sex, or a previous traumatic experience. This can mean your muscles down below go into spasm as soon as you try to have sex, making penetration impossible. These spasms, known as vaginismus, are involuntary; however, the longer they continue, the more sex will be associated with pain. If you're anxious about sex, it might help to talk to a psychosexual counselor, who may recommend using dilators (small, penis-shaped plastic sex aids) to retrain your muscles. Ask your doctor or health practitioner to refer you.

I WON'T LET VAGINISMUS RUIN MY SEX LIFE
Gemma, 24, has had several serious relationships, but has never been able to have penetrative sex.

I first realized there was something different about me when I started my periods, aged twelve. My friends all said they used tampons, but I couldn't seem to get them up inside me. The more I tried, the more anxious I got, until I just gave up. I didn't tell anyone about it, as I was embarrassed, so I kept it to myself and just used pads and towels instead.

The situation got worse when I was sixteen. I'd been seeing my boyfriend for a few months when we decided to have sex for the first time. But however hard we tried, he couldn't get his penis inside me. We were both virgins, so I thought it was because we were inexperienced, but after we'd tried and failed several more times, I realized there might be something wrong. I didn't tell anyone, though—even my mom, who I was very close to. Instead, my boyfriend and I found other ways to enjoy ourselves in bed and we ended up going out for three years without ever having full sex.

After we split up, for reasons unconnected to our sex life, I went out with several other guys. Again, I was unable to have penetrative sex. It was frustrating, but I guess I must have been lucky, as only one of them couldn't handle my "problem." But even that was a blessing in disguise, as it made me realize he wasn't worth it.

When I was twenty-one, I met my current partner, Matt, and finally decided to do something about my problem. I went to my local health clinic and asked to be checked out. They referred me for sex therapy with a specialist counselor.

My first visit to the therapist was incredibly emotional. We talked all about my experiences and feelings, and I was able to be honest for the first time—I found it a lot easier talking to a stranger. During that first session, the therapist told me I had what's known as vaginismus, which is when your vaginal muscles tense up involuntarily, making penetration impossible.

Now I knew what was wrong, I finally plucked up the courage to tell my mom and a few friends about my condition. They were all really sympathetic. I also joined a message group on the Internet for women with vaginismus—I was amazed to find out how many other people have the same problem. I'd always thought I was the only one.

Sadly, just a few sessions into counseling, I moved away, and couldn't continue seeing my therapist. But I was pleased with the progress I'd made, so I've recently found a new therapist in my area. She's great—we practice relaxation techniques and I've been given some exercises to do at home. At the moment, they involve working my muscles down below on their own, but in time, I'll move on to inserting a finger, a tampon and, eventually, maybe even a vibrator.

I don't find it easy—if I try to insert anything in my vagina, I get panicky, my heart races, and I feel breathless. I think my problem is more psychological than physical now— as I'm worried I won't be able to do it, I tense up even more, so I've got to take things one step at a time.

If my vaginismus has taught me anything, it's that there are many more important things in a relationship than penetrative sex. Matt and I have a great sex life—in fact, I have really intense orgasms from manual stimulation, so, although

I'd like to experience the feeling of an orgasm during penetration, it's not the be-all and end-all.

Having said that, I'm going to keep up the therapy sessions, as I still want to experience full sex, and I know I'll probably enjoy it when it happens. More importantly, I want to have children one day. I'm determined to resolve this, and, as far as I'm concerned, it's a matter of when, not if. I'll get there in the end.

WHEN IT'S MEDICAL...

CANDIDA
Candida is caused when the yeast candida albicans, which normally lives happily in your vagina, goes into overdrive, causing a burning sensation, itchiness, and discharge. All this dries out the delicate skin down below, so if you have sex at the start of an attack, or during a mild one, you'll feel sore. Some medicines, nylon underwear, perfumed soaps or shower gels, and sex when you're dry can set off an attack. Treat it with an over-the-counter suppository-and-cream combo, or a one-dose tablet. Get your man treated at the same time and avoid sex again until you're both clear, or you'll pass it between you.

CYSTITIS
Cystitis is caused by a bacterial infection in your bladder, which makes you desperate to pee, then, when you do, you feel as if you're peeing fire. It can be triggered by drinking too much alcohol, overenthusiastic sex, or stress. To keep it at bay, many sufferers swear by going to the bathroom and having a wash before and after sex, while others drink a daily

glass of unsweetened cranberry juice. If you develop cystitis, try an over-the-counter remedy, drink plenty of water, and avoid alcohol, coffee, and citrus fruit until the symptoms ease. If the pain gets worse, see your doctor for antibiotics.

LICHEN SCLEROSUS

Often mistaken for candida (but much more painful), lichen sclerosus is a skin disorder, which causes itchiness, pale white patches on the skin, and the skin to crack during sex—so many sufferers don't have sex for long periods of time. Aside from the external pain, it can also cause the vulva to shrink in size and the vagina to tighten, making penetration difficult. Experts think it could be linked to an overactive immune system, as it's not contagious and can't be passed on through sex. Doctors often misdiagnose it as candida or eczema, so if your symptoms continue for over six months, ask to be referred to a gynecologist or dermatologist, as you may need to have a biopsy under local anesthetic to be sure. There are several treatments you can try, and while it stays in your system for life, the symptoms will often go into remission and disappear, and you'll get your sex life back.

I'VE LEARNED TO LIVE WITH AN INCURABLE DISEASE
Donna, 29, has continual vulval itching, caused by lichen sclerosus.

Until I was twenty-four, I had no major problems down below. In fact, my boyfriend, Sam, used to say how "pretty" my vagina was—it was a bit of an inside joke between us.

But not long after we got married, I noticed a persistent itch in the vulval area. It was in a very definite spot, on the right labial lip, just where the smaller inner lip began. It came on quite suddenly, and the itching was unbelievable—imagine the worst mosquito bite, and multiply it by 100. The itching tended to be worse at night and kept me awake, although it could be pretty fierce first thing, too—it drove me insane.

I put off going to the doctor for six months, as I was too embarrassed. I didn't even tell Sam how bad it was—I just wore cotton underwear and used Vaseline to relieve the itching when it got too bad. One day, though, I scratched it so hard I drew blood—that's when I booked a doctor's appointment.

However, the doctor was pretty dismissive and just gave me some candida cream. To be honest, I suspected he was wrong, but I was just relieved to have a diagnosis. But the itching continued—it might be mild or nonexistent for a few weeks, but then flare up again. It was particularly bad during my period.

After a year, I noticed some white, smooth, shiny patches of skin on my vulva in the area that itched most intensely, as well as some dark discoloration, as if the area was bruised. I panicked—did I have cancer? Was it catching? I'd only had one other serious boyfriend apart from Sam, so was positive it wasn't sexually transmitted. By now, I'd told Sam, who was incredible about it, but I was beginning to feel very self-conscious about what was going on and it was starting to affect our sex life. Although penetration didn't hurt as such, I didn't want Sam to go down there in case it was catching, or the look of my vagina put him off.

Eventually, I decided to see a doctor again. Luckily, a new female doctor had joined the practice and she referred me to a gynecologist. She took a biopsy, to test for a skin condition called lichen sclerosus. The good news was that it wasn't life-threatening, sexually transmitted, or even contagious. The bad news was there's no cure. No one's sure what actually causes it, but sufferers have an increased likelihood of developing vulval cancer, as well as disfiguration caused by scarring of the tissue.

For me, the most devastating thing was the fact I'd be stuck with the itching forever. I was gutted. The gynecologist prescribed me Trimovate ointment—a steroid cream similar to those used to treat eczema. The best I could hope for was to manage the itching by applying it twice a day for three months to get the condition under control. After that, I just used it as I needed it. I still see my gynecologist once a year, just to make sure the condition hasn't got worse, or I haven't developed any signs of vulval cancer.

Although lichen sclerosus isn't life-threatening, it has affected my quality of life. Thankfully, I now know how to manage the itching so it doesn't take over: I stick to cotton underwear (or none at all if I'm at home—Sam loves that!) and I avoid really tight clothing. Fortunately, it's possible for the condition to go into remission for a while, but until that happens, I'm just learning to live with it.

TRICHOMONIASIS

Pronounced "Tric-o-moan-ass," this is caused by tiny parasites, which live in your vagina, but can get out of hand and cause irritation, a fishy smell, and greenish discharge (nice!). During an attack, penetration is too painful to consider, and the smell will probably put you—and your man—off. Visit your doctor or health clinic for anti-biotics, and avoid sex until you're cured.

PELVIC INFLAMMATORY DISEASE (PID)

This is a serious infection of your reproductive system, often caused by a sexually transmitted disease, like chlamydia (see below). Symptoms can take a long time to appear, however. In the early stages, you may feel a dull ache in your abdomen during or after sex. Eventually, you'll feel a deep, throbbing pain when you're aroused, sex will be painful, you might also feel sick and have a temperature. PID is treatable with antibiotics, but if it goes untreated, it may affect your fertility, so if you're worried, see your doctor right away.

CHLAMYDIA

Also known as the silent STI, because it can lie dormant and symptomless for several years, chlamydia is the most frequently reported bacterial STD in the U.S. It is estimated to affect one in twelve sexually active young women, so if you've ever had unprotected sex—even once—you could be at risk. If it goes untreated, chlamydia can cause problems, like lower abdominal pain, pelvic inflammatory disease, ectopic pregnancy, and infertility. The good news is, getting tested is easy—see your doctor or health clinic, buy a test over the counter, or ask for a test the next time you're having a Pap smear. If the results are positive, all you need to clear it up is a two-week course of antibiotics.

HERPES

There are actually two types of herpes virus—type one, which is carried by an eye-opening 100 million Americans, and usually shows itself as facial cold sores; and type two, which is less common, and can appear as genital sores and blisters. Three-quarters of people who carry it never realize they have it, because they show no physical symptoms at all, but if you're unlucky enough to develop blisters, they're often incredibly itchy and painful. Herpes can be passed on whenever the virus is present on the skin, or when a blister or cold sore comes into contact with a break in the other person's skin—so, if you have unprotected sex with someone with blisters, or your man has a cold sore and performs oral sex on you, it's possible you'll contract the genital herpes virus. Despite what you may have heard, condoms are effective protection against herpes as long as they fully cover the affected area; however, experts say it's still not a good idea to have sex until the blisters have healed. Besides, you'll probably be so sore down below you won't want to.

VULVODYNIA

Made famous in *Sex and the City,* when Charlotte claimed, "My vagina is depressed," the word "vulvodynia" literally translates as "painful vulva"—and that's exactly what sufferers experience. It can come on suddenly, and causes a burning or itching sensation in your vulva. Although the cause is unknown, it's thought it happens when the nerve endings in your vagina get irritated or damaged; sex, tampons, tight clothing, or regular bouts of candida can make it worse. The pain can be constant or intermittent, and vulvodynia can disappear as mysteriously as it arrived. Thanks to the pain, and the fact vulvodynia can make you feel quite low and moody, sex will be the last thing you'll feel like. However, it's not contagious and there are treatments available, such as antihistamines to reduce the itching. In extreme cases, doctors can prescribe you low doses of antidepressants.

I WAS GIVEN ANTIDEPRESSANTS FOR MY VAGINA Lauren, 29, avoided sex for four years because of her vulvodynia.

Five years ago, I woke up in the middle of the night in pain. There was a red itchy patch in my vulva. The pain drove me so crazy, I scratched until the area bled. The next day, I was in so much agony I was barely able to walk. I visited my doctor, who diagnosed candida and prescribed antibiotics.

Five weeks later, though, the pain was just as intense. In desperation, I contacted a gynecologist I'd seen mentioned on a herpes website, as it was the only place that mentioned vulval pain.

By the time I got an appointment, I was going out of my mind. Before, I'd been active and loved exercising, but the pain made cycling or even jogging impossible. After examining me, the gynecologist said I had vulvodynia, which causes chronic pain at the opening of the vulva.

Unfortunately, it isn't curable. I was prescribed antidepressants to numb the nerve endings in my vulva, and for a short while, they helped—but they also made me tired and unable to think clearly, so I stopped taking them. Then, as modern medicine didn't seem to be working for me, I tried acupuncture. After several weekly sessions, amazingly, my condition slowly began to improve.

I didn't have sex for four years because of the pain down below. It was hard telling men that while I wanted to sleep with them, it was sometimes impossible, as my vulva would swell and bleed.

I now have acupuncture once a month, which helps control the pain, and I follow a strict diet. I avoid tight clothing, and I've found a way to sit on the back of my tailbone, which lessens the pressure on my vulva. I'll always have to be careful, but that's a small price to pay for being pain-free.

ENDOMETRIOSIS

This is when cells, similar to the ones that line the womb, grow elsewhere in your body. They respond to hormonal changes in the same way your womb does—each month, they grow and bleed like a mini-period. However, unlike a normal period, the blood can't escape, so over time, scar tissue and cysts buildup, and sex can become painful. Sadly, it can't be cured, but the symptoms can be lessened and managed. Drugs can minimize pain and shrink the growths, or they can be removed by laser treatment or surgery.

VESTIBULITIS

This condition causes pain and inflammation around your vestibule—the area where the vulva meets the vagina. Some women find their vagina becomes ultrasensitive, so tight clothing, tampons, or even the lightest touch is painful, while others can just about tolerate penetration. Doctors aren't completely sure what causes it, although it's been linked to candida and cystitis, and isn't contagious. Treatments include physiotherapy, psychosexual counseling, and local anesthetic gels or creams to use before sex.

SEX HURT SO MUCH IT MADE ME CRY
Vestibulitis left Lisa, 22, in severe pain and unable to have sex for two years.

I was nineteen and had been seeing my boyfriend, David, for eight months when my problems began. Around the time I started college, I had a really bad attack of candida. I went to see my doctor and was given a prescription for a one-step tablet, which seemed to clear everything up.

From then on, nearly every time David and I had sex, I'd get candida afterwards. Sometimes, it was mild and I could ignore it, but other times it was so bad I'd have to go to the doctor. Before long, I was having an attack at least once a month, even though I wore cotton underwear and made sure David treated himself too. Nothing seemed to clear it up completely.

After several months, the area around my vagina was dry and cracked, and it even bled. It got to the stage where it hurt to go to the bathroom or wear jeans. But whenever I went to a doctor, they just repeated the original diagnosis and prescribed the usual candida treatments. Looking back, I'm annoyed I didn't stand up for myself, but they were the professionals, after all.

Obviously, my relationship with David was affected. When we tried to have sex, it hurt so much, I'd cry. It got so bad, I wouldn't even let him kiss me, as that could lead to something else, and I was afraid of the pain.

But, instead of going back to the doctors, I just denied I had a problem. I thought if I blocked it out, I wouldn't have to deal with it. David could see something was really wrong and begged me to get help; but as far as I was concerned, I had candida, I was taking the treatment, and that's all there was to it. I felt incredibly lucky David stuck by me, because as far as sex was concerned, I just didn't want to know.

After a while, the pain was so bad, I went to a health clinic, as I reckoned they'd be more used to dealing with this kind of problem than my doctor. They gave me another internal examination and swab test, both of which were excruciatingly painful, but again, diagnosed candida. When I explained it also hurt to have sex, I got the impression they thought I was making it up.

It continued like this for the next two years. During this time, I convinced myself I could live without sex or intimacy. But it did bother me. It was weird going out with my friends, *because after a few drinks, the conversation would turn to sex and I'd just sit there feeling jealous, thinking, "If only you knew what I'm going through." I didn't tell them; it was nice to escape from my problems for a while. I didn't want people to feel sorry for me. I just wanted to be normal.*

By the time I was twenty-one, things had become rocky with David. He'd been patient, but was understandably beginning to question whether I still loved him. I tried to reassure him I did, but he couldn't understand why I wouldn't let him touch me. I think he wondered if it was somehow his fault.

Perhaps this was what spurred me into action. I began to look on the Internet and came across a website for the Vulval Pain Society. I contacted them and I can't explain the relief: they knew instantly what I was talking about. It felt great to be believed.

The Society helped me find a doctor in my area who specialized in vulval disorders. When she examined me, she said I was so red and sore, she was surprised the health clinic hadn't investigated further. She'd seen lots of women with the same symptoms, and I remember thinking, "Yes! Finally, someone understands." The doctor suspected I had vestibulitis, which means your vestibule, the entrance to your vagina, becomes painful when anything tries to penetrate it.

To be sure about the diagnosis, however, I needed to clear up my candida once and for all. I was prescribed an incredibly strong course of treatment, which involved using a suppository every morning and night for two weeks. It was fantastic; my candida completely disappeared. After that, I had further treatment to repair the damaged tissue, using a special cream.

As the specialist suspected, once my candida had disappeared, I was left with a secondary pain, which she diagnosed as vulval vestibulitis. I'd assumed candida was the reason I found sex painful, but, while everything else was now back to normal, I still had a sharp, bruised feeling if I tried to put anything inside me, whether it was a penis, finger, or tampon. The specialist said there were several vestibulitis treatments, but every woman's different and it would be a case of finding the right one for me.

Her first suggestion was counseling. Although vestibulitis is a recognized physical illness, having associated sex with pain for so long, I needed to bring my mind back in touch with my body. The counselor made me realize I'd become depressed by the pain and this had led to me losing my sexual desire. Apparently, lots of people blame vulval problems on a low sex drive, saying women make it up because they don't like sex, but it's not true. I had a high sex drive before this— I only stopped wanting sex because it hurt.

As well as counseling, I tried other treatments. Research suggests foods high in oxolate (a chemical compound found in tea, coffee, chocolate, and root vegetables) can make vestibulitis worse. So, I cut them out. I'm a real chocoholic, so I found it difficult, but I was willing to try anything. Sadly, it didn't have much effect. I tried acupuncture, too, but it was too expensive to pursue.

When I finished college a few months later, I went on a course of Amitriptyline, a type of antidepressant. While it didn't stop the pain, it did help me get some sexual desire back, which was incredible. I was still scared, and whenever David and I tried to have sex, all I could think about was how much it would hurt. But after a while, I found myself looking forward to going to bed. I got really into kissing and touching again, and while the pain was still there whenever we tried penetration, David and I concentrated on other kinds of stimulation, and I began to enjoy myself sexually for the first time in years.

I've recently started a course of physiotherapy, called Biofeedback. Basically, you're attached to a monitor that shows you the difference in muscle movement when you contract and relax your muscles. Part of the reason I find penetration painful is because my muscles have been contracted for so long, because of the pain. I'm hoping sex will become even better if I learn how to relax my muscles.

In the last few months, my sex drive has gone from strength to strength. David and I can do anything we like in bed now, except penetration, and I'm hoping that's just a matter of time. When we do manage it, I know it's going to be fantastic, as we're so experienced at everything else! My vestibulitis has brought us closer together, because we've had to be so open about everything. Most men would have run a mile in a situation like this, but David has been wonderful. He didn't have to stay, but he did, and I love him all the more for it.

Some women don't get a diagnosis for nearly ten years, because their doctors or health clinics don't know enough about vulval disorders, like vestibulitis. I don't want anyone to go through years of pain like I did, thinking it's their fault or all in their mind. I'd urge anyone with problems like mine to go to their doctor and refuse to take no for an answer. It is an illness, and if your doctor can't help, they should refer you to someone who can. Whatever you do, don't ignore it. The main thing I've learned in all this is that it's easy to take your sex life for granted. I didn't realize just how important mine was until it was taken away from me.

Chapter 12
SAFETY FIRST

WHY GREAT SEX = SAFE SEX

Believe it or not, the contraception you choose is as important a factor in your orgasms as the man you sleep with! Reaching your sexual peak is all about letting go and throwing non-sexy thoughts out of your head—so it stands to reason that if you're worrying about getting pregnant, or catching a sexually transmitted infection (STI), your mind isn't going to be on the job in hand. In fact, contraception concerns can be some of the biggest climax-killers going.

Part of the problem for many women is that the contraception we choose doesn't fit either our lifestyle or our sex-style. We often go for whatever method or brand we're first prescribed, then stick with it regardless of whether it's really right for us, because we don't want the hassle or embarrassment of swapping. But not only can a less-than-perfect kind of contraception send your libido into free fall, but many of us are putting up with painful periods, water retention, and problem skin, when these side effects could be easily sorted with a switch to another method or brand.

That's why, just as you wouldn't buy the first pair of shoes you saw when out shopping, you shouldn't necessarily take the first birth-control option a doctor or family-planning clinic suggests. Amazingly, there are over a dozen types of contraception available besides the Pill, yet only

8 percent of women use them. As for the Pill itself, there are over twenty different brands available, yet most doctors prescribe only five. So, if your contraception is coming between you and your climax, you really don't have to suffer in silence. Follow this guide to find the type of contraception that fits you, and your sex life, like a glove.

THE PILL

This little tablet contains two hormones, estrogen and progestogen, which work by stopping your ovaries from releasing eggs; the sperm from reaching the egg by thickening the mucus from the cervix; and the egg from settling in the womb.

Effectiveness: Almost 100 percent (as long as you remember to take it, of course!).

It's perfect if: You're in a monogamous relationship. The Pill puts you in total control of your fertility and means you can have sex whenever you want without worrying about getting pregnant. Used correctly, it's the most effective form of contraception going. And if you're unlucky enough to suffer from PMS or heavy, hellish periods, it could help ease your symptoms, too. Thinking of ditching the condoms? A 2006 survey by condom makers Durex found a worrying one in ten people have, or have had, an STI, so go for a full sexual health exam at a health clinic first, and take your man. Once you've both been given the all clear, you can lose the rubber raincoat!

Steer clear if: You've just started seeing a new man. He may seem the perfect gent, but let's face it: you don't know where he's been—or who he's been with. When you know you're safe from pregnancy, it's very tempting to "forget" to use condoms, but you could leave yourself open to catching an STI. You're not alone—the Durex survey found a scary 52 percent of people admitted to having unprotected sex without knowing their partner's sexual history—however, that's no excuse for not using protection. Also, it's an incredibly small risk, but the Pill has been linked to thrombosis, so if you've got a family history of this, talk to your doctor.

Orgasmic potential: ♤♤♤♤ if you're in a stable relationship and don't suffer any side effects; H if you experience any side effects, such as water retention, weight gain, or a lowered libido. If this is the case, see your doctor about switching to another brand with a slightly different blend of hormones—there's bound to be one to suit you.

THE CONDOM
A thin rubber or polyurethane sheath, which traps sperm inside and stops it coming into contact with an egg.

Effectiveness: 98 percent, if used correctly.

It's perfect if: You're having fantastic sex with a new man. There's only one way to have all the casual sex you want, and stay protected from both pregnancy and infections like HIV, chlamydia, and gonorrhea—and that's always to use condoms. Get adventurous with them and make safe sex saucy by incorporating putting a condom on as part of fore-play—then they don't have to spoil your fun.

Steer clear if: You're sometimes tempted to take a risk. Condoms are very safe, but only when used correctly—and if you don't always remember to use one, can be easily per-suaded to skip them, or get so carried away you only put it on at the very last minute, or halfway through sex, the 98 percent success rate is meaningless. If you're in a monog-amous relationship and want to be in total control of your fertility, it could be time to change to a more suitable method.

Orgasmic potential: ♣♣♣♣ for almost any kind of sex-ual relationship.

THE MINI-PILL OR PROGESTOGEN-ONLY PILL (POP)
This type of Pill contains only progestogen, which works by thickening the mucus from your cervix, making it difficult for sperm to move. It also thins the lining of your womb, so it's less likely to accept and hold on to a fertilized egg.

Effectiveness: 99 percent (again, as long as you remember to take it).

It's perfect if: Those "shock horror" Pill headlines freak you out. The Mini-Pill contains no estrogen—the hormone which has been linked to breast cancer scares. It's a safer choice if you're a smoker, too, as your risk of heart attack or blood clots is less, and it's not as likely to send your blood pressure soaring as the ordinary Pill. If you're in a steady relationship, you might have met your perfect match.

Steer clear if: Your life is one big rush. The Mini-Pill is only as good as the woman who uses it, as you have to take it at exactly the same time every day—even when you've got your period. With most brands, if you're more than three hours late, you could fall pregnant (although some new brands now offer a more user-friendly twelve-hour window). So, if you have a job with irregular hours, or a busy social life, it might not be worth the risk.

Orgasmic potential: 👍👍👍👍 if you're in a long-term relationship and your middle name is "reliable"; 👍 if you're likely to panic if you miss a period occasionally, as this is a common side effect.

THE CONTRACEPTIVE PATCH

This sticky patch, similar to a bandage or nicotine patch, was launched in the U.S. in 2002. It delivers two hormones, estrogen and progestogen, through your skin, which stop your ovaries from releasing eggs; sperm from reaching an egg by thickening the mucus from the cervix; and an egg from settling in the womb.

Effectiveness: 99 percent, if used correctly.

It's perfect if: You like the idea of the Pill, but keep forgetting to take it. You're not alone—an estimated 40 percent of women forget to take one tablet per cycle, while 22 percent miss two per cycle. If this sounds like you, the patch could be the solution, as you have to remember it only once a week, rather than once a day (with one week off in four, when you'll have a period). Slim enough to be worn discreetly underneath your clothes, it'll even stay in place when you're swimming or in the shower. As the hormones reach you through your skin, stomach upsets such as food poisoning won't affect it. Oh, and when you take the patch off, you're fertile again straight away.

Steer clear if: You're a bit self-conscious. Although the patch is flesh-colored, it's about the size of a small matchbox, so if you wear it on your abdomen, upper body, or the top of your arm, it's likely to be seen when you wear skimpy clothing or on the beach. If you're overweight, it may not be as effective, and if you have sensitive skin, there's a chance it could itch. The risks are very similar to the Pill, in that it's been linked with a slightly increased chance of blood clots.

Orgasmic potential: 👍👍👍 if you're confident in bed and don't mind your man catching sight of it (well, you could always claim it was just a bandage...)

THE CONTRACEPTIVE INJECTION

The hormone progestogen is injected into your bottom (lovely!) every two or three months, which stops you ovulating (producing eggs). It also thickens mucus from the cervix, making it difficult for sperm to move through into the womb. In addition, it makes the womb lining thinner, so it's harder for the womb to accept an egg.

Effectiveness: 99 percent, as long as you don't miss an injection.

It's perfect if: You keep forgetting to take the Pill or you don't like patches. One jab gives you a season's worth of protection, without the daily or weekly bother of remembering contraception. Most brands safeguard against pregnancy for eight to twelve weeks. The injection has some health benefits too, and may help protect against endometrial cancer, ovarian cysts, and ectopic pregnancy, although it's best used in a long-term relationship, as it won't protect you against STIs.

Steer clear if: You want a baby soon. Do you find yourself drooling more at Baby Gap's window displays than grown-up Gap's these days? Then hold off on this one. Each jab lasts three months, is irreversible and it can take up to a year before your fertility returns to normal. Because the hormone can't be removed from your body, you might be stuck with any side effects for months, such as headaches, acne, weight gain, mood changes, or disrupted periods.

Orgasmic potential: 👍👍👍👍 if you're in a stable relationship, don't suffer any side effects, and have no desire to hear the pitter-patter of tiny feet any time soon; 👍 if you're feeling broody, or have suffered side effects while using other kinds of hormone-based contraception.

THE CONTRACEPTIVE IMPLANT
A doctor or clinic nurse fits this cunning, small, flexible rod (which is about 1.38 inches long) under the skin in your upper arm. It works by emitting the hormone progestogen, which stops your ovaries releasing an egg each month. It also thickens your cervical mucus, so sperm find it difficult to "swim."

Effectiveness: 99 percent. It's perfect if: You want to fit it and forget it. If you don't want the hassle of having to think about contraception, you can rest easy—once the implant is in your arm, you can forget about it for three years. If you change your mind, it can be taken out at any time, and loses its effect immediately after being removed, so your fertility returns to normal right away. However, it's best used in a monogamous relationship, or in conjunction with condoms as, like the Pill, it doesn't protect against STIs.

Steer clear if: You're a worrier. Launched in the 1990s, implants are still relatively new, so no one knows what any long-term effects might be. One original brand was taken off the market in 2001, when demand fell after users reported side effects including endless periods or none at all, skin problems, hair loss, and mood swings. Current brands claim to be less problematic, but are inserted under local anesthetic, so won't suit anyone with a fear of needles. If you're overweight, the level of hormone released into your body may not be strong enough for it to work; and if you're not in a stable relationship, you'll need to use condoms as well, as it doesn't protect against STIs.

Orgasmic potential: 👍👍👍👍 if you're in a monogamous relationship; 👍 if you're terrified of needles, or are likely to worry about it.

THE FEMALE CONDOM

A thin, soft, polyurethane pouch, which looks like a normal condom, but is bigger. It's fitted into your vagina before sex to act as a physical barrier and trap sperm inside.

Effectiveness: 95 percent. It's perfect if: You can treat it like a sex toy. With an inner ring for extra vaginal sensation and an outer one to rub your clitoris, some fans say female condoms should have a place in every saucy girl's toy box.

Steer clear if: It's just one big turnoff. After sixteen years, the female condom has never really taken off—could this be due to the fact it looks suspiciously like a tiny plastic garbage bag?

Orgasmic potential: 👍👍 if you're able to use your imagination; 👍 if you can't get past its looks.

THE INTRAUTERINE DEVICE (IUD) OR COIL

A small T-shaped plastic-and-copper gizmo, fitted into your womb by a doctor or clinic nurse, which prevents sperm meeting an egg, or surviving in the womb or fallopian tubes.

Effectiveness: Up to 99 percent. It's perfect if: You're a kid-free zone. If you don't want to start a family yet, or already have one and don't wish to add to your brood, the coil is the ultimate solution. Having it put in isn't the nicest ten minutes you'll ever spend, but once fitted, depending on the type you opt for, there's no need to worry about getting pregnant for three to ten years.

Steer clear if: You have more than one partner, as this could increase the risk of infection and could, in severe cases, leave you infertile. If you're squeamish, you may find having it inserted slightly painful. Research also suggests women may have difficulty in getting pregnant immediately after it's removed.

Orgasmic potential: 👍👍👍 if you're in a monogamous relationship and don't suffer any side effects; 👍 if you regularly suffer from heavy or cramping periods, as it can make some women's periods even heavier or more painful. And then sex will be the very last thing on your mind!

THE RHYTHM METHOD

This method works by simply avoiding sex on the days when you're ovulating, and therefore most likely to get pregnant. Mini-computers and urine-test sticks are available to help make the process a little more scientific, but to be honest, even then it's a bit of a gamble.

Effectiveness: Fans claim it's over 90 percent effective if done correctly; however experts estimate it's closer to 75 percent, and a scary one in four couples will become pregnant using this method.

It's perfect if: Your cycle is as regular as clockwork, you're in touch with your body, and having a baby wouldn't be the end of the world. The rhythm method is also favored by women for whom other kinds of contraception go against their religious beliefs.

Steer clear if: You don't have a regular partner and are worried about catching an STI; you don't want to get pregnant; your cycle is often all over the place. It's also not a good idea if you like spontaneous sex, or are easily led by your hormones. As your estrogen levels are highest during ovulation, you'll often feel sexiest at this time of the month—yet this method means you'll be unable to have sex when you want it the most.

Orgasmic potential: ♣♣ if you're in a monogamous relationship and secretly want a baby; ♣ if you know you'll be worrying about pregnancy or STIs during sex.

THE DIAPHRAGM AND CAP

These are physical barriers made from soft, thin rubber. You insert one into your vagina before sex, where it covers the cervix and stops sperm from swimming up into your womb. The diaphragm is beanie-hat-shaped; the cap is smaller, resembles a large thimble, and goes in further.

Effectiveness: 92-96 percent, if used in conjunction with spermicide.

It's perfect if: You hate the way condoms interfere with the sensation of sex, and can't take the Pill for health reasons. You can put the diaphragm in hours before you have sex, so if you're on a promise, you can get ready earlier and save interrupting the moment. Neither the diaphragm nor the cap has any side effects because no hormones are involved. They're environmentally friendly, too, as your diaphragm is made to measure and can be reused over and over again for years.

Steer clear if: You're spontaneous, or have lots of late-night, drunken sex. Both the diaphragm and cap need to be put in correctly, otherwise they won't work, and they need to go in before you have sex—so if you're after a sudden, frantic session, they can put a dampener on proceedings. Also avoid if you enjoy marathon sessions, as the spermicide needs to be topped up after several hours, or if you have sex more than once. The diaphragm can aggravate cystitis, and doesn't suit yo-yo dieters, as weight changes of more than seven pounds could mean you need a different size.

Orgasmic potential: 👎 👎 👎 if your sex life runs like clockwork; if you like spontaneous or drunken sex; love to do it more than once a night; often suffer from cystitis; or are a celebrity-diet fan. Er, that'll be most of us, then!

IN AN EMERGENCY

From condom breakages and missed Pills, to forgetting in the heat of the moment, most women have a contraception crisis at some point. If you think you might have put yourself at risk of pregnancy, there are two kinds of emergency contraception available.

The Emergency Pill:

Also known as the Morning-After Pill, this contains the hormone progestogen, which either prevents your body from ovulating or stops a fertilized egg from settling in your womb. It can be taken up to seventy-two hours after sex, but the sooner you can get to your doctor or family-planning clinic (who'll prescribe it for free) or drug store pharmacy (where you can buy it over the counter), the better. It's 95 percent effective if taken within twenty-four hours, but this drops to 58 percent effectiveness after two days. You might feel sick after taking the Emergency Pill, and your next period may arrive slightly earlier or later than usual.

Copper IUD (coil):

This device, which can also be used as a contraceptive in its own right, is fitted into your womb by a doctor. It releases a tiny amount of copper into your body, which increases the number of white blood cells in the cervix. This knocks out any sperm before they reach the egg. The coil can be fitted up to five days after unprotected sex, and it's proven to prevent 98 percent of pregnancies. Possible side effects include a period-like pain for a couple of days after it's fitted.

Remember: while there is emergency contraception to prevent pregnancy, there is no quick fix to prevent the transmission of an STI if you have had unprotected sex with an untested partner.

CHANGING MY PILL SAVED MY SEX LIFE

Rebecca, 24, couldn't understand why she suddenly wasn't interested in sleeping with her boyfriend—until she checked her contraception.

I'd met Nick three years before at a party, when I was twenty-one and in my first year of university. We immediately hit it off and moved in together after just six months. At first, we had an extremely active and enjoyable sex life. We had sex about four to five times a week, and were both happy with our sexual relationship. One of the reasons our sex life was so good was our ability to discuss our needs and desires with each other. I knew friends who couldn't bring themselves to discuss sex with their boyfriends, but Nick and I could tell each other exactly what we liked.

I'd been on the Pill since I was twenty years old. I'd suffered from bad skin, and my doctor recommended one particular brand to help. I took it with no qualms, and within three months my skin had cleared up a lot. Of course, it also meant Nick and I didn't have to worry about me getting pregnant.

After two years together, our sex life tapered off slightly, but I knew this was normal. We still had sex regularly and we were both always enthusiastic. There was no routine to our sex life, so neither of us were ever bored or felt we were just going through the motions. We were both pretty adventurous, which kept the spark alight.

However, the autumn I turned twenty-three, sex really started to take a backseat. I'd begun my final studies at the university. Nick was also working long hours at his job, so we were both tired and stressed. More and more, I found I wanted to go to bed for a good night's sleep, not to fool around.

After almost two years of a healthy sex life, I suddenly wasn't bothered about sex at all. It wasn't an overnight occurrence, but when I realized Nick and I hadn't had sex for almost two weeks, I was surprised, and then worried. For the first time ever, I hadn't initiated nor shown any interest in having sex with my boyfriend.

At first, Nick wasn't too perturbed. He was also tired from working long hours, so the drop-off in our sex life wasn't noticeable, or a problem. But then I realized I was feeling apprehensive about even the thought of having sex. I really had to make a concerted effort to show interest in sex if Nick instigated things, and although I still enjoyed sex, I didn't lose myself as much. I wasn't able to switch off fully the way I could previously. As time went on, I became more and more aware of the long gaps that appeared in the regularity of our sex life.

I think something that saved our relationship was that we were still very touchy-feely with each other, even though we weren't having sex. We would always hold hands and be affectionate; however, whereas before a night of hugging and kissing on the sofa would have naturally led to sex, now it was all we did. Once or twice, when Nick approached me to have sex, I rejected him and made up an excuse that I was tired. Luckily, he was understanding, but, of course, my rejection affected him. He became much more nervous about broaching the subject of having sex and, instead, let me take the lead. As I wasn't feeling very sexual, I tended to initiate it less and less.

Over time, I went from wanting sex five times a week to dreading the thought of it. In fact, I could barely summon up the will to do it once a month. I couldn't work out what was wrong.

After about three months of this, Nick brought up the subject of our sex life. He wasn't accusing or pointing a finger at me, but said he'd noticed I'd shown little interest in sex. We discussed whether our relationship had actually just come to a natural end, which was scary and upsetting, but we knew we loved each other and wanted to be together. I was worried the spark had disappeared, but Nick put my fears to rest, by saying we were still so loving towards each other, our relationship must be very strong. He put it down to stress, but I felt there was something else adding to my loss of libido, so I did some research on the Internet.

One article I read mentioned the side effects of the Pill. I found out almost every Pill cites lack of sexual desire as a possible side effect. It was exactly what was happening to me. Suddenly, I felt relieved—I knew this was the most likely cause of my flagging libido.

I went to see my doctor, who was quite unhelpful. He explained that lack of sexual desire was indeed a common side effect of the Pill, but there wasn't much I could do about it. He recommended I change my contraception to a new estrogen-based Pill, as low levels of estrogen are linked to loss of sex drive. I took his advice, but as the new Pill's effects could take three months to kick in, in the meantime I tried other ways to boost my libido. I bought some patches on the Internet, which are supposed to increase your sex drive by emitting a sensual aroma.

Slowly, my sexual desire returned. I was surprised, and Nick delighted, by my renewed eagerness to have sex. Now, several months later, our sex life has returned to normal. I feel better about us as a couple, and also about myself—it's like a weight has been lifted.

I know lack of sex can be a difficult subject to discuss with your partner, so I feel extremely lucky Nick and I were able to get through this. I think so many women keep their feelings to themselves when it comes to sex. If you can't talk to your partner, then I'd suggest talking to your friends for advice. It's likely they've felt the same at some point. And definitely try another type of Pill, because it may just make all the difference.

As for Nick and I, we intend to spend the rest of our lives together, and I know that, in the future, any problems we do encounter will be easy to solve because we've overcome one of the biggest hurdles any couple can face.

OVER TO YOU...

I asked five women to confess how their contraception affects their sex lives:

I'm allergic to normal rubber condoms—I get incredibly itchy and develop a red rash down below, whenever they come into contact with my vagina. But as I'm not in a relationship at the moment, I like the security they give me, so I use polyurethane ones instead, which are no problem at all. They're way more expensive, but I suppose you can't put a price on enjoying sex.
NINA, 26

I was on the Pill for six years, but it was starting to affect my sex drive, so I switched to the IUD. It's incredible—after just a couple of months, I got my libido back, and as I've absolutely no wish to have kids just yet, it suits me perfectly.
JAYNE, 25

I've never liked the idea of putting hormones in my body, so I use a diaphragm. I know it sounds a bit old-fashioned, but popping it in before sex only takes a second. It suits me perfectly because it's entirely natural, and my husband likes it because he doesn't have to wear condoms. So, everyone's a winner!

EMMA, 31

My best friend got pregnant while she was on the Pill, and even though she says it happened because she wasn't very good at taking it, it's made me a bit paranoid. So, I use both the Pill and condoms now. I know it sounds a bit over the top, but it makes me happy, and means I can really let myself go in bed without worrying about the consequences.

BECCA, 22

I used the contraceptive implant until a few months ago, when my boyfriend and I decided to try for a baby. I got pregnant just a few weeks after having it removed—I couldn't believe it was that easy! Once I've given birth, I intend to have another one inserted—it's incredible, as it means you can be as spontaneous as you like in bed, without worrying about remembering to take pills or buy condoms.

AIMEE, 29

Chapter 13
ORGASM LIKE A PRO

MY BEST EVER ORGASM...
I always thought you needed fabulous surroundings to have fabulous sex. I used to spend so much time lighting candles and buying expensive massage oils. So, it was a shock when I lost count of how many orgasms I had when my boyfriend and I got busy on a single bed, surrounded by pictures of Bob the Builder. We were in the bedroom of my friend's four-year-old son, who was staying with his grandparents at the time. It just goes to show miraculous sex can happen in the most unexpected places!
    KATE, 29

PRACTICE MAKES PERFECT

Now you've read this book, where do you go from here? The most important thing to realize is that while orgasms are fantastic, like everything in life, they can always be improved upon. And working out how is half the fun of having sex. There are always new things you can try, new positions to get into, and new ways to get turned on. It's all about trial and error, and being willing to experiment—an open mind is one of the most crucial factors in reaching the big O. Remember, every woman is different, and your orgasms are unique and personal to you—there are no rights and wrongs. If one particular technique or tip doesn't give you fireworks down below, at least you've had fun trying! Take things in stages, and always stay positive—mind-blowing orgasms will be yours in time... promise!

ORGASM FACT VERSUS FICTION

It's hard to have an open mind, though, if you still have questions. Clitoral erections, female ejaculation, hour-long climaxes—so much about orgasms is still so shrouded in mystery, it can be tricky to separate fact from fiction, and it's easy to get misled. So, to set the record straight once and for all, here's the truth behind the top orgasm myths:

ORGASMS ARE GOOD FOR YOU
Fact. Orgasms are just what the doctor ordered—they lift your mood, boost your immune system, reduce your risk of heart disease, and bust stress. They can even help you sleep more soundly. So, what are you waiting for? Prescribe yourself one today!

HOUR-LONG ORGASMS ARE POSSIBLE
IF YOU WORK AT IT
Fiction. Most experts agree it's not possible to have orgasmic contractions that last an hour. However, some women find it possible to have several orgasms in a row, a phenomenon known as multiple orgasms. What's the secret? Continue stimulation after the first orgasm, and your body will return to the plateau phase, rather than tailing off.

Tantric-sex fans believe it's possible to have extra-long orgasms by clearing your mind, gazing into your lover's eyes, and slowing your breathing. For tips on special breathing techniques, see page 131.

WOMEN CAN EJACULATE LIKE MEN
Fact. An eye-opening 40 percent of women have ejaculated during orgasm at some point in their lives. Experts used to believe this was due to a leaky bladder (nice!), but it's now believed the liquid ejaculated is similar to male prostate fluid—one of the main ingredients of men's ejaculate. It's nothing to worry about—it just means you've had an exceptionally good time.

IT'S DAMAGING TO GET AROUSED, BUT NOT HAVE AN ORGASM
Fiction. You might feel frustrated if your man heads to the bathroom at the crucial moment, but it won't hurt you. Some women feel tense if they don't orgasm, but this feeling will fade. Men are also unharmed by not having an orgasm—no matter what he may tell you about blue or bursting balls!

WELL-MATCHED COUPLES ALWAYS COME TOGETHER
Fiction. While no Hollywood sex scene would be complete without simultaneous crashing orgasms, only a few couples ever achieve this. So if you've never managed to come together, don't worry. Many couples say they prefer to watch their partner at the moment of climax—something they can't do properly if they're having an orgasm at the same time.

IT'S POSSIBLE TO HAVE AN ORGASM AND NOT FEEL ANYTHING

Fact. Bad news: a very small number of women go through the motions, even having contractions, but feel none of the sensations of orgasm. There's usually a physical or mental reason, and the problem can be solved by visiting a gynecologist and/or a sexual psychologist. Ask your doctor or health clinic to refer you.

IF YOU CAN'T ORGASM, SOMETHING'S WRONG WITH YOU

Fiction. Nearly all women—in fact, 99 percent—can orgasm. They just might not realize it. Using the tips and advice in this book, and keeping on trying, either through masturbation, or with a patient partner who's willing to experiment, is your best bet for hitting the jackpot.

IT'S POSSIBLE TO HAVE AN ORGASM WITHOUT BEING TOUCHED

Fact. Many experts say the brain is our biggest sexual organ, and mental stimulation alone is all some of us need to climax. Some lucky women can orgasm just by thinking sexy thoughts, even at work. It's not a great idea to do it at your desk, though!

A SNEEZE IS A FIFTH OF AN ORGASM

Fiction. A sneeze is a very complicated process, but doctors have never found any link between that and having an orgasm. Shame.

TOO MANY ORGASMS ARE BAD FOR YOU

Fiction. Hooray!

ULTIMATE ORGASM TIPS

So, now all you need to do is take the guidance and suggestions within the pages of this book and build on them, giving you the new, orgasmic sex life you've always craved. Need further inspiration? Here are ten top tips to intensifying your orgasmic experience, just to get you started...

1. DO SOMETHING DIFFERENT

Variety really is the spice of life when it comes to orgasms. If you usually tense or pull in your muscles when you come, try pushing them out, instead, for a feeling of wild abandon. Or, if you normally speed up your breathing, try taking deep, slow, regular breaths.

2. SET THE ALARM A LITTLE EARLIER

Okay, so you might feel half asleep, but apparently the best time for sex is first thing in the morning. Your hormone levels and his testosterone levels reach their peak at around 9 a.m.—so pull a sick day, pull the duvet over your head, and get your man to push all the right buttons!

3. MAKE EYE CONTACT

It's tempting to shut your eyes when you're about to come (especially if you're fantasizing about George Clooney at the same time), but looking deep into your man's eyes during climax can make it even more intense for both of you.

4. CLOSE YOUR LEGS

Some women find that keeping their legs close together during sex gives them stronger orgasms, as it means the clitoris gets much more attention during penetration. Why not give it a go?

5. GIVE YOURSELF A HELPING HAND

As you climax, try covering your clitoris with your cupped hand, resting the tips of your fingers just inside your vaginal opening. Then, pull upwards slightly, putting gentle pressure on your pubis (where your pubic hair meets your vagina). The added pressure and tension should help to make your orgasms stronger and more satisfying.

6. STOP SMOKING

The nicotine and tar in tobacco restrict blood flow to your genitals and lower your testosterone levels, playing havoc with your sex drive. Experts have found that people report more and better orgasms after they've kicked the habit.

7. SEE THINGS FROM A DIFFERENT ANGLE

Just as you're about to come, move over on the bed slightly, so your head hangs over the side. The sudden rush of blood to your head should give you a very different kind of rush down below!

8. REACH YOUR PEAK

A few seconds before you climax, get your man to stop whatever he's doing for a few seconds, before starting up again (you can do the same if you're masturbating). Do this several times. This technique, known as peaking, builds up extra tension in your nethers—all of which makes for a hit-the-ceiling orgasm when you finally allow yourself to let go.

9. BE PREPARED

Before indulging in bedroom action, gently press on the area two to three inches below your stomach button for a few minutes. This cunning trick helps to increase blood flow to your vagina and give your climax a little extra oomph.

10. FORGET ABOUT IT!

The more you think about having an orgasm, the less likely it is to happen. Stop seeing it as the be-all and end-all of sex, and just enjoy yourself for a change. That earth-shattering, world-altering climax will hit you completely out of the blue!

"WE'RE GOOD IN BED!"

To prove it's possible for any woman to fulfill their orgasmic potential, I asked four self-confessed sex goddesses, all of whom give themselves ten out of ten in the bedroom, to share their secrets to sex success...

SEX SECRET: BODY CONFIDENCE
Camilla, 22, has been with her boyfriend for six months.

For me, a great sex life stems from one thing: confidence. Feeling good about your body, whatever shape or size you are, is a bigger turn-on than any sex toy! When I was eighteen and first started having sex, I used to have all the usual body hang-ups most girls have. Does my butt look big? Are my boobs too small? Do I smell strange? I even used to sleep in a tank top, as I felt too shy going naked. But, over time, I've learned to love my body—imperfections and all.

My turning point came when a long-term boyfriend dumped me. Becoming more independent helped boost my confidence, which then transferred to my sex life. I think giving birth to my little boy helped, too. I was convinced, as soon as I became a mom, my sex life would be over. But being a mom makes you realize life's too short to worry about what you look like. In all honesty, the man you're with is glad to get you naked. The last thing he'll notice is your wobbly body. If he didn't want you, he wouldn't be in bed with you in the first place.

Learning to be happy with my new body improved my sex life beyond belief. The minute I relaxed and ditched those hang-ups, sex got better and better. I soon felt comfortable enough to ask for what I wanted in bed. Just saying, "Actually, I'd prefer it if you did it this way," has finally allowed me to get the sex I've always wanted.

And, now, it couldn't be better. I love spontaneous sex, and refuse to fall into a routine. I love surprising my man in a sexy nightie or "accidentally" dropping my towel when I get out of the shower. Seeing the look on his face when I give him a naughty treat is a huge turn-on. I like to have sex when and where the desire takes me. I'm fairly open to new things, which, I think, comes from confidence. It also means things are never boring.

I used to be so worried about how I looked, or whether I was pleasing my man, that I forgot about the most important thing—enjoying sex! I used to be mortified in embarrassing situations, like having trapped air. Over time, I've learned to laugh about it. Not worrying about silly things has helped me lose my inhibitions and gain confidence. That's a surefire way to feel sexy naked.

CAMILLA'S TIPS:

1. Don't do it in the dark. He's in bed with you because he finds you sexy, so don't cover up—flaunt it!
2. Do laugh off those embarrassing moments. They happen to everybody.
3. Do be spontaneous. Sex doesn't always have to be saved for bedtime; surprising each other on the spur of the moment can be a huge turn-on.

SEX SECRET: HAVING FUN

Stephanie, 20, has been with her man for two years.

The most important thing to remember about sex is it's supposed to be fun. You have to enjoy yourself, otherwise, what's the point? I never take sex too seriously. That's when it becomes boring and you stop enjoying it. It doesn't matter if you don't orgasm every time. People put too much emphasis on that. It's the learning process that's half the fun.

Variety is definitely the spice of my sex life—trying new things keeps the excitement up. Sex is all trial and error, so don't be scared of making mistakes. I used to think I'd feel silly talking dirty, for example. I was terrified I'd say something cheesy. So, the first time I tried it with a man, I tested the water by whispering sexy thoughts in his ear. I kept my voice low, under my breath, so, if it turned him off, it wouldn't be such a big deal. But he loved it! And I'm glad I took the plunge because I discovered a whole new turn-on. That gave me the confidence to try other new things.

Sometimes, it's just making little changes. I once kept my heels on and that was great fun. And I love flirty dates with my man, too. We both know what's going to happen when we get home, so we spend all evening building up the tension. I don't think seduction should ever stop, no matter how long you've been in a relationship.

Foreplay can often be more fun than sex itself. Playing naughty games can last for hours without it having to lead to full sex. I was painfully shy when I was younger, but meeting somebody I can have fun with has changed all that. Communication is a vital part of a healthy sex life. That's why I openly talk about sex with my man, in and out of bed.

Confidence doesn't come from a man you're with; it has to

be from you. There's a lot to be said for using your imagination. I've often had fun with food or toys in the bedroom. You might feel silly about suggesting something, but I'd say, go for it. Chances are, he'll be as excited as you. And you might find a fantastic new turn-on for both of you. Yes, there will always be embarrassing moments. But when you can both laugh about them, you're on to a winner.

STEPHANIE'S TIPS:

1. Don't always obsess about having an orgasm. Concentrate on enjoying yourself and the rest will happen naturally.
2. Keep your sense of humour in bed. If you can laugh, even when something goes wrong, it'll keep the fun in your sex life.
3. Use your imagination. You'll be surprised the fun you can have with everyday things like food. Who needs sex toys?

SEX SECRET: PREPARATION

Jennifer, 25, has been with her boyfriend for eighteen months.

People often forget amazing sex doesn't just happen—you have to make an effort. My boyfriend regularly works away for long periods of time, which has helped us make a real effort, even when we're not physically having sex. But it's a good trick for anyone to learn—the longer your foreplay, the more explosive the sex when you finally get to have it. Anticipation is a big turn-on.

While my boyfriend's away, we'll share sexy phone calls and send each other naughty texts. It keeps us going until we see each other again. Then, when we do, the sex is always out of this world. Every time we have sex, it feels like the first time all over again.

I love to surprise my man when he gets home. So, I'll help create a really sexy atmosphere by lighting candles and running us a nice hot bath. Then we might treat each other to a massage. Spontaneous sex is great, but I think putting in a little preparation is well worth it. The longer you wait for it, the better sex can be.

It's helped me to build a trusting and strong relationship with my man, too. We're both very open and happy to talk about what we both like in bed. The steamy long-distance phone calls certainly rack up my phone bill, but they're the best foreplay in the world. Using your imagination and talking sexy with your man is better than any complicated position or technique you can try.

It's vital to feel as sexy as you can, too, and that's why I think it's important to pamper yourself. You can do this in loads of ways, but my guilty pleasure is saucy underwear. I have over one hundred sets of bras and panties, from cute, girlie ones, to vampy, risquè pieces. There's nothing sexier than knowing you have some gorgeous undies on underneath your outfit. Plus, my man always gets a nice surprise! I think you should do whatever makes you feel confident—whether it's spending time on your hair and makeup or wearing lovely clothes. I often go out and get a manicure or have a beauty treatment to make me feel good and put me in the mood for sex.

I believe in the saying, "You get out what you put in." And when it comes to sex, I think the more you invest in it, the better it'll be. Good sex doesn't just happen; you have to make an effort. For me, it's all about quality, rather than quantity.

JENNIFER'S TIPS:

1. Focus on foreplay. It doesn't always have to lead to full sex; building the anticipation with week-long foreplay makes for an explosive ending.
2. Don't let the romance fizzle out. Lighting scented candles, sharing a bath, and giving each other massages all help to keep sex a sensual experience.
3. Pamper yourself to feel your sexiest, whether it's new makeup, a new hairstyle, a manicure, or splurging on new undies.

SEX SECRET: EXPERIMENTING

Elizabeth, 20, has been in a relationship for two-and-a-half years.

The only way to stop things going stale in the bedroom is to reinvent your sex life constantly. For me, that means always trying something new. I never let sex get routine. If you feel like you're going through the motions and not getting the most out of your sex life, you know it's time to change things.

Over time, I've learned the only way to get what I really want in bed is to ask for it. When I first began having sex, it often felt like a chore. I wasn't particularly getting anything out of it and just thought, "It has to be better than this." The few men I'd been with simply weren't interested in my pleasure. But at the same time, I didn't have the confidence to change things for myself. That was until I met my current boyfriend. Suddenly, I started thinking, "What would I really love from my sex life?" That's when I decided to take control.

At first, I felt nervous about asking for something specific in the bedroom. But I eased myself into it by using a subtle approach. I would say things like, "Wouldn't it be fun if we tried this?" There's always that awkward doubting feeling

*where you're left wondering, "What if he thinks I'm weird?"
But it didn't take me long to gauge his reactions and I soon
found out he was as turned on as I was about experimenting.*

*Being in a loving, trusting relationship helped me come out
of my shell, too. It gave me the confidence to suggest things I'd
never have dreamed of before. Even if it's just making small
changes to your sex routine, trying new positions or experimenting with technique. Small changes can make a big difference.*

*Now, my man and I often role-play and dress up in the
bedroom. Living out our fantasies is like an escape from everyday life, which helps me lose my inhibitions. I'd say, if you're
comfortable with it, try anything once. It'll add a new dimension
to your sex life. If you don't take things too seriously, sex will
remain fun.*

*Sex has always been a bit of a talking point amongst my
friends, which I think made me more comfortable discussing
it with men. Now, I'm completely open to saying what I don't
like in bed and asking for what I do.*

*The nicest thing about my current relationship is we're
constantly learning about sex together. If you feel comfortable
with a man, it shows in the bedroom. Getting to know each
other's turn-ons is all part of the fun. And if you don't try
these things, you'll never find out what does it for you and
what doesn't!*

ELIZABETH'S TIPS:

1. Aim to try something new every time you have sex.
   Even if it's just varying your positions or the time of
   day you do it.
2. Be adventurous. You don't have to swing from the
   chandeliers, but if you have always had a secret desire
   to try something new, go for it.
3. Don't be afraid to tell your man exactly what you want.
   After all, if you don't ask, you don't get!

Chapter 14
WHAT'S YOUR ORGASM IQ?

MY BEST EVER ORGASM...
*I know I'm incredibly lucky, but all my orgasms are amazing.
I couldn't single out just one. I love trying new things in bed,
and whenever I see a magazine with sex tips in it, I have to
buy it. That's the key to having incredible orgasms—you've
got to be willing to experiment.*
SUZANNE, 24

TIME TO TEST YOUR KNOWLEDGE

You've read the book, so you should be on your way to being a bit of a pro at this climaxing lark—but just how much do you really know about the big O? Take this quiz, and discover if you're ready to have your best sex ever.

THE QUESTIONS

1. TRUE OR FALSE? THERE ARE TWO DIFFERENT TYPES OF FEMALE CLIMAX—VAGINAL ORGASMS AND CLITORAL ORGASMS.
   A. False. All orgasms are caused in the same way—by nerve stimulation.
   B. False. There are three types of orgasm—vaginal, clitoral, and anal.
   C. True. But vaginal orgasms are more powerful.
   D. True. But clitoral orgasms are more powerful.

2. IS TAKING VIAGRA THE BEST WAY TO INCREASE YOUR ORGASMIC POTENTIAL?
   A. Yes. It works on your vagina in the same way it does on his penis, by increasing blood flow.
   B. Yes. It relaxes you and releases feel-good hormones, which help get you in the mood.
   C. Yes. It contains chemicals that'll stimulate your brain and give you multiple orgasms.
   D. No, because it's not designed for women to take.

3. WHAT'S THE AVERAGE LENGTH OF TIME WOMEN NEED TO BE STIMULATED BEFORE THEY'LL ORGASM?
   A. One-and-a-half minutes.
   B. Five minutes.
   C. Twenty minutes.
   D. At least an hour (and with some men it'll never happen).

4. IF YOU CAN'T FIND YOUR G SPOT, ARE YOU JUST NOT LOOKING HARD ENOUGH?
   A. Yes. Everyone has a G spot—and you'll have incredible

orgasms if it's stimulated correctly.

B. My what? I've no idea where I might have left it, but it's probably with my car keys.

C. No. It hasn't been proven that every woman has one.

D. No. Some women's G spots are too far up inside their bodies to be stimulated by hand.

5. WHICH SEXUAL POSITION MAKES ORGASMS MORE LIKELY FOR WOMEN?

A. A long, slow screw up against the wall—just like the cocktail.

B. The Coital Alignment Technique (CAT).

C. The missionary position.

D. Any position performed underwater.

6. HOW MANY WOMEN USUALLY COME THROUGH INTERCOURSE ALONE?

A. 95 percent.

B. 75 percent.

C. 50 percent.

D. 25 percent.

7. IF YOU USE A VIBRATOR REGULARLY, ARE YOU LESS LIKELY TO CLIMAX DURING SEX?

A. Yes, because you'll dull the nerve endings in your clitoris.

B. Yes, because your body will learn to respond only to a certain type of stimulation, and fingers will begin to seem too slow.

C. Yes, because your man's penis will no longer feel substantial enough when he's inside you.

D. No, it won't make any difference to your orgasms in the slightest.

8. YOU FIND IT DIFFICULT TO ORGASM WITHOUT A HOT AND STEAMY FANTASY RUNNING THROUGH YOUR MIND. THIS MEANS:

A. You don't really want your man, and need a saucy scenario to focus on.

B. You're normal—many women need to fantasize before they orgasm.

C. You're a bit strange, and could do with going for counseling.

D. You're not satisfied with your sex life and would secretly like to act out your fantasy for real.

9. HE'S BEEN RUBBING YOUR CLITORIS FOR WHAT FEELS LIKE HOURS, BUT YOU JUST DON'T FEEL TURNED ON. THIS IS PROBABLY BECAUSE:

A. There are communication problems in your relationship, and you and your man's wires are getting crossed.

B. Your clitoris may not be fully developed, so you can't get turned on properly.

C. His fingers are too big, and your clitoris is too small.

D. He's using far too much lubrication.

10. WHAT'S THE BEST WAY TO HAVE A MULTIPLE ORGASM?

A. There's no such thing—it's a myth originally invented by dubious porn directors.

B. Take things very slowly, stop just before you come, then start to build things up again.

C. Have sex for at least an hour, to buildup the sexual tension properly.

D. Get into certain sexual positions, like doggie style.

THE ANSWERS

1. A

There's no scientific proof that there are different types of orgasm. You climax when the nerve endings around both your clitoris and vagina are stimulated for long enough— in fact, you don't have any nerve endings beyond the first three inches of your vagina, which kind of negates the longer-penises-are-better theory (read chapter one to learn exactly how your climax works). But, while there aren't two separate pleasure centers, there are different strengths of orgasm, depending on the kind of stimulation you're experiencing (vaginal or clitoral), your emotional state, and how tired you are.

2. D

Scientists are working on female Viagra, and if they bring it out, it may well offer spectacular results. But right now, the only kind available isn't designed for women to use. Viagra works on the purely physical problem of erectile dysfunction, and women's sex-drive problems are usually caused by something different, such as tiredness, stress, lack of lubrication, or depression. So forget pills and potions—if you want to liven up your libido, a glass of champagne, a massage, or a new vibrator is a better, much safer idea. See chapter three for more ideas to get your batteries charged up without resorting to medication.

3. C

Of course, all four answers can apply, but, on average, it takes twenty minutes to get women sufficiently worked up to have an orgasm. Unless you're so breathless with passion one brush of a finger sets you off, your man will probably need to devote at least twenty minutes to foreplay before you're adequately turned on. If he's rushing things, slow him down by stroking him gently in return, or teasing him by touching his penis and then backing off (see chapter four for more suggestions). When you do eventually have sex it'll be explosive, and he'll have had plenty of time to make sure you're really in the mood.

4. C
Despite all the hype about the G spot, most sexperts now agree it's debatable whether every woman has one. The G spot is a little, spongy, bean-shaped area on the front wall of your vagina, and many women can reach it with their fingers or specially shaped vibrators (see chapter five for how to start your search). Others, though, have been up there for days with torches and a search party, and come back with nothing but numb fingers and battered genitals. So, if you can't find yours, don't panic—you're not necessarily doing anything wrong. In fact, you and your man will have more time to focus on your clitoris, which, when you think about it, is no bad thing at all.

5. B
If you're determined to have an intercourse-only orgasm, one of your best bets is to try the CAT—where your clitoris is stimulated by your man's pelvis as he moves inside you (see page 107 for how to get into position). He lies on top of you and then inches upwards until his pelvic bone is resting right above your clitoris. Then, instead of thrusting, he grinds in circles—which not only stimulates the walls of your vagina, but also works wonders on your clitoris. This way, if he keeps it up long enough (as it were), you may eventually have an orgasm while he's inside you. And if not, at least you'll have had heaps of fun trying.

6. D

Perhaps amazingly, only a quarter of women are lucky enough to have an orgasm through intercourse without any clitoral stimulation. Their luck is probably because their clitoris is closer to their vagina, so it's easier for them to get aroused by the movement of their man's pelvis. For the rest of us, it doesn't matter how long he bangs away, because without direct touch, you may enjoy yourself, but an orgasm will be almost impossible. If you want to up the likelihood of climaxing through penetration, try one of the top-ten orgasmic positions in chapter six, or experiment with a small bullet vibrator held against your clitoris during sex (see chapter seven for inspiration).

7. D

You'd have to use your vibrator all day, day in, day out, for it to make even the slightest difference. Your clitoris is a resilient little thing and using a vibrator to masturbate won't deaden your nerves, make your man's penis seem smaller, or teach it to respond to just one type of stimulation. You might find you come a lot quicker with a vibrator (see chapter seven for how to find one that suits you)—but still, even if your man's tongue has been going for hours, sometimes the journey can be as much fun as the arrival, so to speak. And if you genuinely prefer your flexible friend to your man, it might be a sign he needs a gentle shove in the right direction when it comes to knowing how you like to be touched—i.e. tell him what you'd like in bed.

8. B

Fantasies are incredibly common, as our brains and bodies work best together during sex—just take a look at what some women conjure up in chapter eight! However, this doesn't necessarily mean we'd actually want to act out our fantasies in real life. For example, while you might day-dream about seducing Brad Pitt in the back row of his latest premiere, it's perfectly clear that if you tried in reality, the only physical action you'd get is a fight with his burly security guards. So, if anyone (i.e. your man) assumes you want something to happen for real, you can put him straight quickly.

9. A
It's extremely rare to have physical problems with your clitoris, and while using too little lubrication may be an issue, using too much certainly isn't. For many women, sexuality is tied up with emotions, so if you're having relationship problems, or things are weighing on your mind, you're much less likely to be able to relax enough to come. In a nutshell, it's not the orgasm that's the problem, it's the man—and woman—behind it. You'll need to confront what is going on emotionally before things can get better physically. See chapters ten and eleven for other reasons why your big O may be playing hard to get.

10. B
Multiple orgasms do exist, although they're usually considered to be several orgasms that take place during the same sex session, rather than a ten-minute, crashing-waves experience. The best way to maximize your orgasmic fun is to let him stroke you, very slowly, until you feel the excitement building. When you get to the "plateau" stage, just before you come, he should stop and pull back (frustrating, but necessary). Then, he begins again, gradually building up the tension, then stops, until you can't bear it a second longer—at which point, even the lightest touch will send you over the edge. Afterwards, while your clitoris is still sensitized, get him to start all over again... this time, with his tongue.

You may find your next orgasm is even more intense than the first. Fantastic!

HOW DID YOU SCORE?

Give yourself one point for each correct answer. Then add them up to see if you've hit the big O...

1-3 A BIT OF AN ANTICLIMAX

No wonder your orgasms aren't all they could be. The biggest orgasm obstacle is bad communication in bed, so you need to let your man know what you want. If you can't find the right words, you can help him by gently moving his hand (or mouth) to exactly the right spot. You should also find out what turns you on by getting plenty of masturbation practice. Reread this book, paying particular attention to chapters four, five, and seven. Look on the bright side—as homework assignments go, it could be worse...

4-7 NEARLY THERE

Not bad, but you could try harder. To fulfill your orgasmic potential, try out at least five different positions from chapter six, including the fail-safe CAT from question five in this quiz, to see which works best for you. Reread chapter seven and invest in a good, three-speed vibrator—then teach your man how to use it on you. It'll give his fingers a rest, and if you use lots of lubrication, it'll hugely enhance your sexual fun.

7-10 OH, YES!

It's fair to say you're a bit of an expert, but the good thing about orgasms is there's always room for improvement. Expand your repertoire by trying out all the advanced moves in chapter six; make your fantasies work for you by reading chapter eight; or try to maximize your physical prowess by regularly practicing the exercises and breathing techniques in chapter nine. With your knowledge and new skills combined, you'll be guaranteed explosive orgasms every time. Have fun!

OVER TO YOU...
Who better to have the last word than five women, who reveal the defining moments that unexpectedly changed their sex lives—and their orgasms—forever...

WE TURNED A QUICKIE INTO A SLOWIE
I work in a hotel, and one night I was working at the bar when the most gorgeous man turned up. As the evening wore on and the bar emptied, we got chatting. At the end of the night, he asked me to come back to his room, and as soon as we stepped inside the door, he started slowly undressing me. We began having frantic sex standing up, but then he stopped, picked me up, and carried me to the bed while still inside me. No man had ever shown that much attention to bringing me to climax before. The whole experience taught me great sex doesn't have to be frenzied—it can be slow and sensuous, too. Just thinking about that night puts a smile on my face!
    MANDY, 21

I REALIZED SIZE DOESN'T MATTER
My new man is over a foot taller than me, and weighs seventy pounds more than I do. He's also quite clumsy, so when we first met, I was concerned about what he'd be like in bed. How wrong can a girl be? He was incredibly considerate and put my needs first. He realized we had to adopt different posi-

tions because of our different sizes. Best of all, he showered me with compliments, which made me feel like a total love goddess. I now tell all my single friends that first appearances can be deceiving!

ALICE, 26

WE MADE A PACT TO BE MORE UNDERSTANDING
When my man and I moved and I started a new job last year, our sex life took a nosedive. One evening, I was sitting watching Lost in my towel after having a bath. When my boyfriend came in from work, he immediately knelt down in front of me—but it was too much, too soon. I told him to leave it, and he stomped off. He got upset, saying he was only trying to be spontaneous. As he poured his heart out, I realized I'd been so wrapped up in my own stresses, I hadn't thought about how he was feeling. We made a pact to try to see things from the other person's point of view when it comes to sex, and our love life has improved hugely since.

SARAH, 27

A PORN STAR INSPIRED ME TO TALK DIRTY
My husband and I went to Berlin for a weekend. On our first morning there, we were flicking through the TV channels when we found a porn film. We started watching it, and at first we found it hilarious, as the female porn star was shouting, "Give me cock!" Soon, however, we were getting down to business ourselves. My husband and I started saying filthy things to each other—and discovered we loved it. We were both amazed we found porn such a turn-on, and since then, we often spice things up by talking dirty.

CLAIRE, 25

I OVERCAME MY INHIBITIONS

I'd always been too nervous and, if I'm honest, slightly embarrassed to use a vibrator. Even the thought of buying one made me cringe. That was, until I was given one at a friend's party. One night, a couple of weeks later, while my boyfriend was away, I tentatively opened the box and tried it out. It took a while to get the hang of, but when I did—oh my God—the orgasm I had was incredible. After that, I started using it regularly, and even experimented with lubricant— something else I'd always assumed was "dirty" before. I've learned so much about myself through using my vibrator. While, at the moment, it's just something I do for me alone, I hope to share my new toy with my boyfriend eventually. Who knows what else I'll discover then?

KATE, 24

INDEX

ALSO AVAILABLE FROM AMORATA PRESS

THE BEST SEX YOU'LL EVER HAVE!
Richard Emerson, $13.95
Packed with a variety of new ideas to spice up lovemaking, *The Best Sex You'll Ever Have!* illustrates risque positions, fantasies, role playing, sex toys and erotic games.

EROTIC MASSAGE FOR LOVERS: SENSUAL TOUCH FOR INTIMACY AND ORGASMIC PLEASURE
Rosalind Widdowson & Steve Marriott, $16.95
Designed to help lovers unleash the dynamic potential of the erogenous zones all over the body, this book explores a range of sexually charged movements and manipulations, with some surprising additions and ingenious variations.

THE LITTLE BIT NAUGHTY BOOK OF SEX
Jean Rogiere, $9.95
A handy pocket hardcover that is a fun, full-on guide to enjoying great sex.

THE LITTLE BIT NAUGHTY BOOK OF SEX POSITIONS
Siobhan Kelly, $9.95
Fully illustrated with 50 tastefully explicit color photos, *The Little Bit Naughty Book of Sex Positions* provides everything readers need to start using these thrilling new positions tonight.

MALE MULTIPLE ORGASM: TECHNIQUES THAT GUARANTEE YOU AND YOUR LOVER INTENSE SEXUAL PLEASURE AGAIN AND AGAIN AND AGAIN
Somraj Pokras, $13.95
This book teaches a man how to make love for hours while giving his partner absolute pleasure again and again.

ORGASMS: A SENSUAL GUIDE TO FEMALE ECSTASY
Nicci Talbot, $16.95
Straight-talking and informative, *Orgasms* is a girl's best friend when it comes to understanding the physical, psychological, and spiritual factors contributing to great sex and intense orgasms.

THE WILD GUIDE TO SEX AND LOVING
Siobhan Kelly, $16.95
Packed with practical, frank and sometimes downright dirty tips on how to hone your bedroom skills, this handbook tells you everything you need to know to unlock the secrets of truly tantalizing sensual play.

To order these books call 800-377-2542 or 510-601-8301, fax 510-601-8307, e-mail ulysses@ulyssespress.com, or write to Ulysses Press, P.O. Box 3440, Berkeley, CA 94703. All retail orders are shipped free of charge. California residents must include sales tax. Allow two to three weeks for delivery.